Football in the Land of the Soviets

'Football is an excellent way in to understanding any country,
and if there's one country we need to understand better now,
it's Russia. An extremely timely book.'
—Simon Kuper, co-author of *Soccernomics*

'A fascinating, thorough and at times revealing investigation
into the origins of football in the USSR.'
—Jonathan Wilson, author of *Inverting the Pyramid*

'A fascinating, brilliantly researched insight into the patchwork
origins of the ruthless powerhouse that Soviet football
would become.'
—Robert O'Connor, author of *Blood and Circuses:
A Football Journey Through Europe's Rebel Republics*

Also available

St. Pauli: Another Football is Possible
Carles Viñas and Natxo Parra

'Football has always been tribal, but this book shows how tribalism can be a force for good. Radicalism, social inclusion and joy all have their place on the terraces; there's more than one Marcus Rashford out there!'
—Val McDermid

'A fascinating history of the football club, and explains how politics, music, art and sport combine on the terraces in the fight against discrimination. A powerful and mesmerising book about football, and how it can be a force for good in an often corrupt and capitalist world.'
—*FourFourTwo*

'An engaging history ... it is a tale unlike any other sports team.'
—*CounterPunch*

'A timely reminder of the power of the football club, as a cultural and societal institution, in many ways more powerful than a religious place of worship or a town hall.'
—*Sportsman*

'Less overlapping full-backs, catenaccio and gegenpresse, more punk rock, autonomia and Gramscian theory, this is no ordinary football book.'
—*Football Pink*

Football in the Land of the Soviets

Carles Viñas

Foreword by Toni Padilla
Translated from the Catalan by Luke Stobart

First published in the Catalan language as *Futbol al país dels soviets* by Tigre de Paper Edicions in 2019

English language edition first published 2022 by Pluto Press
New Wing, Somerset House, Strand, London WC2R 1LA
and Pluto Press Inc.
1930 Village Center Circle, Ste. 3-384, Las Vegas, NV 89134

www.plutobooks.com

The translation of this work has been supported by the Institut Ramon Llull

LLLL institut
ramon llull

British Library Cataloguing in Publication Data
A catalogue record for this book is available from the British Library

ISBN   978 0 7453 4744 8   Paperback
ISBN   978 0 7453 4746 2   PDF
ISBN   978 0 7453 4745 5   EPUB

This book is printed on paper suitable for recycling and made from fully managed and sustained forest sources. Logging, pulping and manufacturing processes are expected to conform to the environmental standards of the country of origin.

Typeset by Stanford DTP Services, Northampton, England

Simultaneously printed in the United Kingdom and United States of America

To Lluís 'Pogos'

For always persevering and fighting
making him indispensable

Football is a realm of human freedom practised outdoors.

Antonio Gramsci

Bourgeois sport has a simple and clear purpose: to make man even more stupid than he is … In bourgeois states, sport is used to produce cannon fodder for imperialist wars.

Maxim Gorky

Contents

Abbreviations

BSC	British Sports Club
BSP	British Socialist Party
CDKA	*Sportivnyy Klub Tsentral'nogo Doma Krasnoy Army* / Sports Club of the Central House of the Red Army
CPGB	Communist Party of Great Britain
CPI	Communist Party of Ireland
CSIT	*Confédération Sportive Internationale Travailliste* / International Workers in Sports Confederation
CSKA	*Tsentralni Sportivni Klub Army* / Central Sports Club of the Army
FIFA	*Fédération Internationale de Football Association* / International Federation of Association Football
GPU	*Gosudarstvennoye Politicheskoye Upravlenie* / State Political Directorate
GTO	*Gotov k Trudu i Oborone SSSR* / Ready for Labour and Defence of the USSR
IOC	International Olympic Committee
IWW	Industrial Workers of the World
KFS	*Kruzhok Futbolistov Sokolniki I* Sokolniki Football Players' Circle
KSO	*Klub Sporta Orekhovo* / Orekhovo Sports Club
M16	Secret Intelligence Service
MKL	*Moskovsky Klub Lyzhnikov* / Moscow Lyzhnikov Club
MKS	*Moskovsky Kruzhok Sporta* / Moscow Sports Circle

NEP	Novaya *Ekonomicheskaya Politika* / New Economic Policy
OFV	*Obshchestvo Fizicheskogo Vospitania* / Presnya Society of Physical Education
OLLS	*Obshchestvo Lyubiteley Lyzhnogo Sporta* / Amateur Ski Sports Society
OPPV	*Opytno-Pokazatel'naya Ploshchadka Vsevobucha* / Vsevobuch Experimental Demonstration Site
PTCh	*Pochtovo-telegrafnye Chinovniki* / Postal and Telegraph Employees
RFS	*Rossiyskiy Futboln Soyuz* / Russian Football Union
RKKA	*Raboche-Krestyanskaya Krasnaya Armiya* / The Workers' and Peasants' Red Army
RKS	*Rogozhsky Kruzhok Sporta* / Rogozhsky Sports Circle
ROA	*Russkaya Osvoboditel'naya Armiya* / The Russian Liberation Army
ROWS	*Russkiy Obschtschewoinski Sojus* / Russian All-Military Union
RSDWP	*Rossiyskaya Sotsial-Demokraticheskaya Rabochaya Partiya* / Russian Social-Democratic Workers' Party
RSFSR	*Rossíyskaya Sovétskaya Federatívnaya Social-istíčeskaya Respúblika* / Russian Soviet Federated Socialist Republic
RSI	Red Sport International
SIS	Secret Intelligence Service
SKS	*Sokolnichesky Klub Sporta* / Sokolnichesky Sports Club
SPD	*Sozialdemokratische Partei Deutschland* / Social Democratic Party of Germany
SRS	*Partiya Sotsialistov-Revolyutsionerov* / Socialist Revolutionary Party

SVA	*Svenska Arbetareförbundet* / Swedish Workers Union
SvFF	Swedish Football Federation
TFF	*Türkiye Futbol Federasyonu* / Turkish Football Federation
TsDKA	*Tsentral'nogo Doma Krasnoy Army* / The Central House of the Red Army
TSOVVO	*Tsentralniy Otdel Vseobschei Voennoy Podgotovki* / Central Division of Universal Military Training
TUL	*Suomen Työväen Urheiluliitto* / Finnish Workers' Sports Federation
UDMF	Union for the Defence of the Motherland and Freedom
VSFK	*Vysshiy Sovet Fizicheskoi Kultury* / Supreme Council of Physical Culture
ZKS	*Zamoskvoretsky Klub Sporta* / Zamoskvoretsky Sports Circle

Foreword
Stands Turned into Historical Settings

I had seen them so often in old black-and-white photographs I could not believe there was one a few metres from me. Simply, I had not expected that a symbol of another era would still be alive and well. In a vest that looked too small, a plump gentleman was tucking into a hot dog with a *budenovka* on his head. It was the summer of 2000. Where the old Dynamo Moscow stadium once stood, before being knocked down and replaced by a more modern one, CSKA and *Spartak* were playing a Moscow derby, with the Red Army team (CSKA) fighting to avoid relegation. There were more Spartak fans in the stands, who were separated from their CSKA equivalents by hundreds of police. 'In the away game someone was killed – a knifing', explained a policeman in broken English. You could sense the tension but the big guy with the *budenovka* was still focused on his frankfurter. I could not stop watching him, asking myself why he was wearing that military hat: the *budenovka*. But, I thought, if it made any sense to find that headdress anywhere after the fall of the Soviet Union, it would be in a match with the Army's club.

Since then, I have seen *budenovkas* in the stands every time the Russian team plays. The hat has become yet another Russian symbol. You can buy them in the same places they sell weird souvenirs, such as T-shirts of Vladimir Putin riding a bear, lighters showing Stalin's face, religious icons, and replica AK-47 rifles. Indeed, I even bought a *budenovka* in Belarus, a few metres from what used to be the Dinamo Minsk stadium – another deceased structure (because in its place they built a new ground). In Russia, buildings are raised and razed to the ground in the same location, telling you who rules. Nowadays, money is the ruler, and the new stadiums are luxury ones.

The *budenovka* is a pretty but curious hat, with personality. You could say it looks funny with that spiked hood. Yet when the headgear first appeared, it was in a less-fun context than a football game. The history of the *budenovka* is the history of Russia. The hat was approved as part of the Soviet Army's uniform by a special commission created by Trotsky, in 1918, to bring some sort of order to the troops that wanted to change everything from bottom to top. The semi-rigid pointed cloth helmet with adjustable side flaps was ideal for the cavalry and for cold climates. And it became fashionable thanks to the feats of cavalry commander General Semyon Budyonny, whose name ended up being given to the hat. New headwear for new times. These were the years in which artists who wanted to change and rethink everything – from the structure of the state to household furniture – designed dazzling sportswear that ended up being exhibited in museums. The kits, however, were not successful among sportspeople. Yet, the *budenovka* could still be seen in the stands during the last World Cup in Russia, and quite a few of them. After 1918, it was necessary to rethink sport. And football survived. It is a tenacious sport. A popular religion that has coexisted with Tsars and Soviets.

But in that summer of 2000, which now seems so distant, that solitary *budenovka* cohabited with flags showing royal shields on the imperial colours of white, yellow and black; modern Russian flags; and the odd CSKA flag with Lenin's face printed on red fabric. A kid of around 15 came up to ask for money to buy a match ticket wearing a T-shirt bearing Adolf Hitler's face. Neo-Nazi skinheads shared the terraces with Soviet symbols. Two of the opposing sides in a world war shared the stand, in a mix than was as powerful as it was disturbing. I spent the whole match (which CSKA won 2–1) thinking about Russia's history. And how this has affected its football, to the extent that enemy flags now shared a space. Incidentally, at half-time, a group of granddads came out to wave at everybody. They were the champions of the 1960 European Nations Cup [translator's note: today's Euros] for the Soviet Union. Russia celebrated as if this milestone was purely its own achievement; although there had been three Georgians in the starting line-up, none of them had travelled to receive the homage. History remained so alive in that stadium that it was frustrating that there was then no literature available through which to discover how Russian football had adapted to governmental change.

Football has been just another setting in which this fascinating land's complex history has played out. Politics has always had the capacity to enter every home against the will of its inhabitants. Sport has similarly entered but almost always as a guest. And politics has benefited from its position of power to politicise sport. In few locations has this been so clear as in the Soviet Union. Everything is political, as Gramsci said. And Russian football has always been conditioned by the land's history – as hard as it is fascinating. For many years, Carles Viñas has endeavoured to explain Russian football's past. An exciting journey that few people had taken before. Russia is still the great unknown, making it hard to overcome clichés and fears. Books like this are much needed to be able to fill in the gaps that still exist.

There has always been a wall that has complicated access to Russia, whether this be an iron curtain, a Berlin wall, or the cultural barrier between a Europe that has been suspicious of any country that is as big as a continent. This culture clash becomes clear from the first pages of this book, from the stories of fights involving the first Russian footballers, little willing to be 'gentlemen' like the British they fought with. Scenes that should have been included in the tales by magnificent writers which narrated the changes Russia was subject to in the nineteenth and twentieth centuries, when after vacillating between opening up to the West or staying anchored to almost Oriental traditions, an Empire ended up broken and giving way to a new state that was as brutal as its predecessor. And where sport went from being a tool to being a propaganda weapon. If in the first Soviet years, football was treated with suspicion; by 1930, the streets were covered by posters in which – using that typical Russian imperative – young people were told to '[p]lay football'. The posters – becoming more and more realistic and less and less imaginative as Stalinism progressed – were now raising players' social statuses, despite the state, in theory, aspiring for everyone to be equal. 'Football has become a truly popular sport in our country' said a striking 1947 advert in *Pravda*, when the USSR was ready to defeat the Western states' national teams on the playing field.

Some generations of Europeans – from the United Kingdom to Greece – grew up fascinated by Russian footballers and sportspeople. They came from such an isolated and mysterious world; they could only be devils or bearers of hope. There was a big question mark over what happened inside the USSR. Even if literature helped prise Soviet sport open, it remained a fascinating world in which those giants in red who touched the heavens on winning the 1960 European Nations' Cup were either reviled or admired. This was one of the high points of a national football that started out timidly but which, while the country felt victorious at the end of the Second World War, seemed destined to win the World Cup. All the same, while the USSR shone in the Olympic Games, it never progressed beyond the semi-finals of the World Cup.

Here we have a story of defeats and victories, disappointments and surprises, and lies and sincerity. An ensemble tale revolving around a ball, featuring British businessmen, generals, leaders, and politicians – all of which are major actors in this history of Russian football. From Tolstoy's *War and Peace* to Pasternak's *Doctor Zhivago*, from Bulgakov's *Master and Margarita* to Grossman's *Life and Fate*, the great Russian tales have always been ensemble narratives spread over time and including many often-contrasting views. Their protagonists do not always meet, as has happened in Russian football, which sometimes has better plots than level of game.

Toni Padilla

Introduction

Football came to the Russian Empire at the end of the nineteenth century, ushered in by the industrial development the country was undergoing. In those tumultuous times, the sport established itself: at first, thanks to foreign residents in the country's biggest cities; later, becoming popular among the native population. Football was a sign of the deep changes Russia was going through in the late nineteenth and early twentieth centuries.

To understand the evolution of Soviet football we must delve into the origins of the sport in late Tsarism. In that period, the desire among a section of local elites to modernise and industrialise Russia – understood to bring Russia in line with the Western European powers – helped introduce football into the Empire. Sport was thus a vehicle through which to introduce and accept modernity.

Its appearance, spread, and evolution took place in a tense and constantly changing social context. The collapse of the Russian political system, made worse by defeat in the Russo–Japanese War and later participation in the First World War, ended up aiding the success of the 1917 October Revolution. The fall of the Romanov Dynasty and the creation of the world's first socialist state inevitably helped football bloom and develop.

The existence of these three evolutionary phases explains why this study is structured in three parts – acting as a chronological thread. Each recalls the volumes written by Russian novelist Lev Nikolayevich Tolstoy: *Childhood* (1852), *Boyhood*

(1854), and *Youth* (1857). These seemed suitable to metaphorically refer to the gradual stages through which Soviet football evolved. These went from soccer's beginnings associated with the Tsarist Empire, in which the game was merely a form of entertainment for the local aristocracy and foreign settlers, to the game's transformation thanks to the October Revolution, after which it became a mass popular-class phenomenon. During the whole process, the different figures involved had different stances on the sporting activity. There were members of the Tsarist court who rejected the game for its foreignness, and revolutionaries who defined it as an instrument of the bourgeoisie.

Paradoxically, as we shall see, the war explains why both the Tsarist Empire and the Bolsheviks ended up promoting the sport. The need for physical training to improve the efficiency of troops on the battlefield was crucial to the spread and local rooting of the sport. The defeats suffered by Russia's Imperial troops, and the later creation of the Red Army, would help spread football.

How did this metamorphosis take place? Why did those that disapproved of playing the sport end up instrumentalising it for their own benefit? What impact did the Russian Revolution have on football? Were the clubs politicised before the Bolsheviks' victory? How is it that a bourgeois game ended up as the main hobby of the Soviet working class? These are just some of the questions this volume attempts to answer.

PART I

Childhood

Детство

1

Football Comes to Tsarist Russia

The inception of sport in Tsarist Russia is connected to industrialisation and modernisation, which were understood to be part of helping the Empire catch up with Western Europe. The desire for economic, cultural, and social progress was key to encouraging the arrival of foreigners, who would end up decisively influencing both the playing and organisation of football in Russia.

The balance of forces guaranteeing interrelation between the major European powers was disturbed by the Crimean War (1853–1856). In a context shaped by the weakness of the Ottoman Empire (Turkey), Tsar Nicholas I demanded, with a dispute over access to holy sites as a backdrop, that the Ottoman Sultan protect the rights of his Orthodox Christian subjects. The call was rejected by the Sultan's allies, Britain and France, whose main interest was to avoid Russian expansion in the area. Their reaction triggered intervention by the Tsarist Army, which invaded the Danubian principalities of Moldavia and Wallachia, leading to war being declared and the start of hostilities. The conflict intensified in the Crimean Peninsula, where Russian generals had mustered over 200,000 men to defend Sevastopol – Russia's Black Sea naval base – from a siege by a Franco–British coalition. Eventually, the peace negotiated at the 1856 Paris Congress put an end to Russian territorial ambitions.

For Russia, the consequences of the war were notorious. Nearly half of its troops died in combat. Politically the rout suffered sparked the beginning of a deep crisis for the Tsarist autocracy, which would end by abolishing serfdom, in 1861. It also saw the emergence of a revolutionary movement, at the end of that decade. The Empire was exposed as no longer being a decisive power in Eastern Europe to instead being an unstable, weak, and ineffective country. Nor were reforms attempted by Tsar Alexander II in the administrative, educational, and territorial spheres able to resolve the country's political and economic problems.

The Crimean defeat showed the need to regenerate the Empire.[1] The Tsar attributed the failure to the backwardness

---

1   The defeat revealed the problems caused by having troops poorly trained and malnourished. The effects of the Russo–Turkish War (1877–1878) plus the great famine ravaging the country created great concern over people's state of health in the Empire in the late nineteenth century. Such a context encouraged links to be created between sport and militarism. Key in bringing this about was Peter Franzevich Lesgaft (1837–1909), biologist and Professor of Anatomy at Kazan University (Tatarstan), who strove to spread physical education among the people, while informing the military about his work. After being dismissed from the university for having spoken out against unscientific practices, he began working, in 1872, as a gymnastics-therapy consultant and writing books and articles on the related sport. Three years later, thanks to financial support from the Russian Ministry of War, he travelled to 13 European countries to gain first-hand knowledge of physical-education systems at different institutions, such as the Central Army Gymnastics School at Aldershot or the Royal Military Academy at Woolwich. After he returned to Russia, in 1877, he published his work *Relationship of Anatomy to Physical Education and the Major Purpose of Physical Education in Schools* in which he outlined the programme he wished to apply in the country's military academies. In 1894, he took up being the St Petersburg branch secretary for the Society for the Encouragement of Physical Development. Lesgaft believed in promoting women's participation in sport as a means to their social liberation. At the beginning of the twentieth century, the Tsarist authorities in Finland put Lesgaft under house arrest for having collabo-

of the Russian economic and social system. To overcome the country's slow and deficient industrialisation in the late nineteenth century, the monarch hastened the re-establishment of diplomatic links with Britain so as to improve and expand its own business relations. The prospect of business and other opportunities from investing in Russia aroused the interest of several businesspeople linked to cotton manufacturing in Lancashire (in the English north east), which had emerged as one of the epicentres of the international textile industry. They did not want to miss out on the benefits of investing in a developing country.

Thus, in the late nineteenth century, the Russian government allowed the entry of foreign capital – predominantly from Britain and Germany – with the idea of stimulating and modernising the country's economy. Industrialisation transformed Russian society, which went from being predominantly peasant to having an emerging urban proletariat. This, however, caused large imbalances in a mainly agricultural economic structure such as the Russian, as well as mass migration from rural areas to the big cities,[2] such as Moscow and its surrounding areas.

---

rated with students taking part in revolutionary movements. In 1907, he moved to Cairo for health reasons, dying there two years later. Before, the Imperial Guard had hired as instructor to its officers G. M. de Pauli, who, since 1831, had been the pioneer at introducing Swedish gymnastics in Russia. De Pauli was replaced by a fellow countryman, Carl Frederich de Ron, who, between 1837 and 1858 was responsible for the physical fitness of the mentioned military unit. In 1859, Frederich de Ron published the first *Rules for Army Gymnastics*. Years later, in 1885, the first gymnastics school for officers was founded in St Petersburg. M. O'Mahony, *Sport in the USSR. Physical Culture – Visual Culture* (London: Reaktion Books, 2006), p. 125. On Lesgaft, see J. Riordan, *Sport in Soviet Society. Development of Sport and Physical Education in Russia and the USSR* (Cambridge: Cambridge University Press, 1977), pp. 47–53.

2   In 1905, *muzhiks* (peasants) made up 61 per cent of the country's active population. Insecurity and famine added to already being up to their

It was in this context of emergent industrialisation that the first settlements of foreign citizens were created in the country. The largest community was undoubtedly the British, which settled in the main urban centres, such as St Petersburg, Moscow, and Odessa, but also in other cities and towns controlled by the Russian Empire. Among its constituents were members of the diplomatic corps, textile factory and mill owners, as well as managers, engineers, technicians, and machinists that were hired by Russian employers to transfer their knowledge to native employees. Once in Russia, these Englishmen and Scots – like the Germans – reproduced their preceding recreational habits, among them obviously being football.

As well as modernising the economy, their arrival influenced the physical fitness of the Empire's subjects. For that reason, from the 1860s, Russia proved more receptive to physical education and the new recreational pursuits that had increasingly spread across Europe. These included the German *turnverein* (gymnastics clubs), the Czech *Sokol*,[3] and the

---

neck from trying to pay exorbitant rents and taxes. This forced them to leave the rural areas and move to the big cities to eke out a subsistence.

3   Gymnastics movement linked to Czech nationalism, taking the name of falcon (*sokol* in Czech). It emerged in 1862 as a split from the Gymnastic-Orthopaedic Institute in Prague, taking its inspiration from the German gymnastics associations (*turnverein*), Its initial leaders (*starosta*) were Miroslav Tyrš, art history lecturer at the University of Bohemia, and Jindřich Fügner. Its main aim was to provide the whole of the Czech nation with physical, moral and intellectual education. At first, this was given to men – of all ages and classes – and later women were allowed to partake. Its members wore traditional Czech gym clothes: red shirts and caps with falcon's feathers. *Sokol* groups were created in all those territories with people of Slavic origin, such as Poland, Slovenia, Serbia, Bulgaria, Croatia, and the Russian Empire. The *Sokol* movement, which was characterised by its militarism, had a significant role in the development of Czech nationalism. The routines that its members did were based on discipline and did not require use of sports equipment. They

Swedish gymnastics movement.[4] These activities' contribution to restoring people's physical training interested members of the wealthy classes and the most liberal section of the nobility. All the same, it was foreigners living and/or working in the country that founded the first big-city private clubs, such as St Petersburg Yacht Club[5] and the Muscovite English Club, to do sports such as cricket, gymnastics, skating, tennis, billiards, or sailing. Many of the local elites, however, preferred doing fencing, swimming, hunting, or being spectators at horse or cycle races, boxing or wrestling matches. Even intellectuals were attracted to sport. Figures such as playwright Anton Chekhov or the writer Aleksandr Kuprin actively participated in such – in the Russian Gymnastics Society and the Kiev Athletic Society, respectively.

From 1880, the rise of sport was observable thanks to the proliferation of new clubs. Different sports bodies were founded, including for cycling – the period's most popular spectator sport – but also athletics, boxing, and ice hockey. With regards to football, one of the pioneering teams was

---

did free-handed moves in groups or (pyramid) formations and military exercises (boxing, fencing, wrestling), as well as dances, theatrical performances and hikes. See C. E. Nolte, *The Sokol in the Czech Lands to 1914: Training for the Nation* (New York: Palgrave MacMillan, 2002).

4   Physical education was introduced into Russian schools in the 1870s thanks to insistence by the army. In fact, gymnastics was seen to be a kind of military training. Performing drilled exercises would produce 'a disciplined subject in peacetime and a fearless fighter in war' (according to a key military exponent in Riordan, *Sport in Soviet Society*, p. 20).

5   Founded in 1860, this was the country's first multi-sports organization. Among its members were foreign diplomats living in St Petersburg, and part of the local aristocracy. Following the Victorian British associative model, all those working in manual jobs were banned from joining. In contrast to the city, in Moscow the first local yacht club was not created until 1867. R. Edelman, *Spartak Moscow: A History of the People's Team in the Workers' State* (New York: Cornell University Press, 2009), p. 14.

the Victoria Football Club, created in 1894 by Britons and Germans.[6] Many of these pioneering sports teams were promoted by merchants and industrialists who sought to offer healthy activities to their employees, while, at the same time, gaining some social prestige for themselves.

In those days, football was not the most popular sport in the country by a long way. The one attracting the most attention and spectators was the aforementioned horseracing.[7] Indeed, it became the principal national pastime in Tsarist Russia. Later, the sport that won the most fans from the local elites was tennis, which can largely be explained by it being the royal family's favourite. Other sports to the Romanov's liking were chess and cycling – one of Tsar Nicholas II's biggest passions.

The first sports societies set up in the country, beginning in that era, were yachting and car-racing clubs, linked to the wealthy, and cycling organisations promoted by members of the aristocracy and bourgeoisie.[8] The popularity of cycling – a symbol of modernity – was due to the low price of bicycles (of a hundred roubles[9]) and the fact that no kind of training or

6   Other clubs in which football was played existed prior to this but Victoria was the first to be founded only for this particular sport to be played.

7   Between 1854 and 1907, the number of registered clubs that reared horses rose from 96 to 3,700; and the number of yearly races, from 260 to 3000. The number of racecourses also rose: from 20 to 54.

8   In 1892, there were around forty cycling clubs, such as the Moscow Cyclist Club – founded in 1888. The proliferation of cyclists on the country's city streets caused misgivings among the popular classes, who saw it as infringing on their turf. Thus, in the Strelna district of St Petersburg – a city that, in 1903, had more than 25,000 bike licenses – velocipedists were systematically pelted with stones. In rural areas, peasants would break bottles on pavements to obstruct the path of cyclists. Consequently, the sport laid bare the class conflict emerging in the country. All the same, cycling would soon lose its exclusive sporting character and become identified as a simple means of transport.

9   In 1892, 6000 cycles were sold. Ibid., p. 98.

special facilities are needed to do it. It was very popular among women, skilled workers, and even the clergy. The latter's interest in the sport, however, led the Orthodox Church to disapprove of it, as they saw priests travelling about by bicycle as indecent.

With regards to football, the role of foreigners – particularly Brits – was vital. Without the will to industrialise that opened up Russia to outside investors and skilled workers, it is not possible to understand how football was imported into the country in the last third of the nineteenth century.

2

The British Connection

According to some Russian authors, long before the arrival of the British – the main exporters of football around the world (thanks to them having standardised rules) – a rural game called *kila* or *shalyga* was played in the Russian Empire.[1] This indigenous predecessor to football dates back to the seventeenth century, when Tsar Alexis I, father of Peter the Great, ruled the Empire. The peasants would play it in the summer or winter – even on ice. Two teams of eight or nine players would fight over a leather hair-filled ball the size of a human head. The objective was to get it across the borders of the neighbouring town (*gorod*). When that happened, the members of the team managing this would shout '*kila!*' Despite the aggressiveness of the game, which had little in common with modern soccer, violent conduct was not tolerated. It was not the only pastime in rural areas, where frequently people engaged in skiing, ice skating, hunting, and Russian boxing (*stenka na stenku*). Of course, this range of entertainment had not been in any way codified and consequently differed from rule-based sports. The latter were considered a modern urban phenomenon, alien to the traditions of the Russian countryside.

Apart from these rudimentary instances, playing football as we know it today began in Russia courtesy, as mentioned, of Britons. In order to speed up the industrialisation process, Russian manufacturers decided to hire skilled engineers and

---

1   As recounted by cleric Nikolay Gerasimovich Pomyalovsky in his volume *Seminary Sketches* (New York: Cornell University Press, 1973).

managers from Britain and central-European countries like Germany. These pioneering sporting 'ambassadors' were mainly businessmen, technical staff, or members of diplomatic corps. In its first years, only Britons played in the matches. Soon, Russians would be incorporated, enabling holding matches with the first mixed line-ups. Most of the local residents drawn to football were students, military cadets, or company employees. Foreigners' hegemony over Russian football would persist until 1908, when native Russians questioned being dominated by Germans, English, and Scottish.

Britons, who had gone to Russia in the first half of the nineteenth century to manage and work in the textile sector, created their own communities. They often lived in housing provided by their employer, close to the factories they worked in. These employees were provided with schools for their children and even churches. Furthermore, they later set up social and sports clubs, reproducing the community structure and civil-society fabric of their place of origin. Their members, however, were not the first to play football matches in Russia. In the 1860s, the St Petersburg port and the Odessa naval base in the Black Sea became football's gateway to the Tsar's Empire. In both cities, British sailors from ships docking there played informal 'pick-up' matches on the quays. In 1868, the *Samakat* newspaper reported a match played in St Petersburg.[2]

Most of the Russian elites saw football as a 'strange and crude game' and an 'extremely rough sport'. Likewise, the local press described it as 'an English game with a large ball. Usually played by people with firm muscles and strong legs, someone weak would be hopeless and could only be a spectator of it'.[3] A

---

2   L. McReynolds, *Russia at Play. Leisure Activities at the End of the Tsarist Era* (New York: Cornell University Press, 2002), p. 55.

3   D. Goldblatt, *The Ball is Round. A Global History of Soccer* (New York: Riverhead Books, 2008), pp. 162 and 163.

perception in no way unusual if we take into account that the first match played by Britons in Russia – organised by William Hopper[4] in 1886 – seemed more like a rugby match than a football one. In fact, the game was cut short by the capital's police as they considered it to be 'brutal, and liable to incite demonstrations and riots'.[5]

It was a comprehensible fear if we bear in mind the social context at the time. The rural exodus had encouraged outlying suburbs to sprout up around the big cities, pockets of serious deprivation, and the spread of hunger. And this was on top of the indebtedness of peasants resulting from Tsar Alexander II's agrarian reform (which had a modernising bent but was sterile), growing inflation, and defeat in the Russo–Japanese War (1904–1905, after losing the Battle of Tsushima). The combined result was for discontent to spread. In 1905, the first protests took place. St Petersburg's Bloody Sunday rising took place on 9 January (according to the Julian calendar), calling on the monarch to intervene to solve the problems devastating people's lives. (It was not for nothing that one of the most-chanted slogans was 'freedom and happiness or the

---

4 Hopper was a Scot born in Penicuik – a town near Edinburgh – on 22 June 1816. At 15, he became an apprentice for a textile-mill builders in Berwickshire. In 1838, he moved to Manchester and, four years later, he left for Bolton. There, he worked for Benjamin Hick, who, the following year, sent him to Russia to supervise the engineering required for a cotton-manufacture plant belonging to the firm Egerton Hubbard & Co., which was being built near to St Petersburg. The following year, he worked in Moscow at the Mazourin mill until, in 1847, he joined forces with a man called Wrigley to create a smelting plant (Shipock Iron Works) and a small textile mill. Two decades later, he would become the sole owner of the business, and his three children began working at the firm. In 1882, just before his death, he created a company, W. Hopper & Co., with his offspring as partners.
5 K. Baker, *Fathers of Football: Great Britons Who Took the Game to the World* (Durrington: Pitch Publishing, 2015) p. 55.

grave'.) This ended in a bloodbath at the gates of the Winter Palace. Yet the autocracy had been openly challenged. Even though the revolt was repressed, it was a warning of what would come after.

3

St Petersburg – Russian Football Capital

In 1703, (Tsar) Peter the Great founded a city on the site of the Neva Delta's marshes, aiming for it to be 'Russia's window to the West'. The construction of the city, as well as responding to the will to build bridges with Western Europe, would also benefit strategic and business interests. Russia's access to the sea was blocked in the Black Sea by the Ottoman Empire and to the north by the ice that prevented ships from reaching the port of Arkhangelska – near to an estuary on the White Sea. St Petersburg was to provide a way out to the Baltic Sea and, additionally, a counterbalance to Swedish military might. In fact, its creation was made possible after, on 4 May 1703, Russian troops snatched the Ingria fortress from the Swedish Army at the mouth of the Neva River. This victory was part of the war in the Baltic provinces (1702–1707), one of the conflicts making up the Great Northern War (1700–1721), which ended in the signing of the Treaty of Nystad, Swedish defeat, and the confirmation of Russia as a major world power.

Little over a week after conquering the Swedish military enclave, the Tsar ordered a fortress to be built on the nearby Zayachy Island – towards the right bank of the Neva – in order to control the estuary. This is how, on 16 March 1703, St Petersburg was officially founded. While war continued, thousands of Russians were forced to move there to build the city, under the supervision of German engineers invited to participate by the Tsar himself. In 1712, St Petersburg was formally made the capital of the Empire, replacing Moscow.

Nearly two centuries after its creation, St Petersburg became the route through which football entered and penetrated the country. Specifically, dating back to the 1860s, its port – alongside that of Odessa – was the point of entry. British sailors on boats moored in both locations were the first to play informal matches. There is evidence that a decade later, in 1879, the first formal match was played between teams made up of English employees at St Petersburg's two biggest factories: Sampsonievsky and Nevsky.[1]

The city had a greater inclination than Moscow to bridge gaps with its equivalents in Western Europe. Thanks to its large foreign-settler community, it adopted Western forms of popular culture, which it believed were inherent to modernisation, among which naturally included football. Ex-pats were thus the true pioneers in Russia, not just of football but of other sporting activities.

It was these foreigners that had come to manage firms or work in the diplomatic corps or textile retailers or factories who organised the first casual matches. Some of them were part of the Nevsky Cricket, Football, Hockey, and Tennis Club – one of the city's ground-breaking sports societies. Shortly after, similar organisations were founded such as *Nevka* – the Scottish Circle of Amateur Footballers[2] – *Gloria* – made up of English college students – *Germania FC* – consisting of the

---

1 Cotton-manufacture factory founded in 1843 and located in the Rozhdestvenskaya district. It was one of the first mechanised plants in St Petersburg.

2 The clubs used the Russian word '*lyubitel*', which can be translated as both 'lovers' and 'amateurs'. For this reason, most included the word in their official name.

Putilov Works' German employees[3] – and the *Victoria* Football Club – created in 1894 by English and German residents. At the beginning, these clubs reserved the right of admission to British or other foreign citizens settled in St Petersburg. This, plus the fact that football was a sport introduced by 'foreigners', caused some resentment among those Russian citizens denied the right to play and join such societies. It was not until 1890 that, tired of restrictions and obstacles, homegrown Russians decided to found their own teams. Later, they even created mixed teams in which Russians and foreigners would play side by side. The first account of a match played by Russian players is from 1892, during a break in a cycling competition taking place at the Semyonov Hippodrome. It was a match without a referee or written rules and included participants who hardly knew how to play football. The following year, in 1893, the first 'public' match with spectators took place, being held at the Semenovsky Square velodrome.

A few years later, on 15 July 1896, the first football club only consisting of Russians was created: St Petersburg's *Kruzhok*

3   Created in 1868 by the Russian industrialist and engineer Nikolay Putilov, the Works were devoted to producing railway rolling stock. By 1900, the plant had 12,400 employees. The company worked for the Russian government, producing artillery equipment for the Imperial Army. By 1917, it was the biggest firm in St Petersburg. That year, on 18 February, the workers at the plant began a strike that sparked the February Revolution. It was not the first time that the factory workers called a stoppage to demand their rights, having downed tools in 1905. Twelve years later, in the middle of the First World War, the situation in Petrograd became extremely serious. Lack of goods and resources pushed up prices. Workers consequently demanded better wages. Over 100,000 workers went onto the streets to make their demands heard. After the revolt, the company was renamed *zavod Krasny Putilovets* (Red Putilovite Plant) and produced the first Soviet factors. In 1934, after Sergei Kirov, leader of the Leningrad Communist Party, was assassinated by a gunman, the plant was renamed again as the Kirov Plant. During the Second World War, it produced the KV-1 tank.

Lyubiteley Sporta (Circle of Amateur Sportsmen). The origins of 'Sport' – as the club became popularly known – go back to 1888. Then, Pyotr Pavlovich Moskvin,[4] together with a handful of students, small businesspeople, and public servants created the Circle in Tyarlevo (just outside St Petersburg), which originally focused its activity on athletics. Eventually, in 1896, the authorities approved the club's constitution, the moment from when it took on its final name (St Petersburg Circle of Amateur Sportsmen).

The first match played in Russia that followed English Football Association rules was held in 1896 on Krestovsky Island. Its promoter was Georges Aleksandrovich Duperron, a key figure in the development of Russian sport.[5] On 24

4   In 1945, Moskvin was honoured as Grandmaster of Sport of the Soviet Union for his vital role in the development of athletics and sport in general in the country. Three years later, he was one of the victims of the earthquake that, on 6 October 1948, devastated Ashgabat – capital of Turkmenistan – and killed 110,000.

5   Born in St Petersburg on 12 September 1877 and descending from a family of French merchants that settled in Russia in the early nineteenth century, Duperron was one of the Russian football's biggest promoters. He went to St Peter's School (*Sankt-Petri-Schule*) – St Petersburg's German school. Later, he studied law at St Petersburg University. An early sports fan, at the age of 14, he rode in horse races held in the Russian capital's Yusupov Park. During a trip to France in 1895, he came into contact with local cycling societies and participated in different competitions in this field. Back in Russia, he combined his studies with doing sports such as riding, track and field, hockey and football. Duperron was a promoter of the St Petersburg Circle of Amateur Sportsmen. He took it on himself to translate the British football rules into Russian – creating the first such translation. In 1901 he became – alongside John Richardson – one of the organisers of St Petersburg's first football league: then called the Autumn Cup. He also took part in founding the first Russian football federation, which included 54 sports clubs. Between 1912 and 1917, he was the body's representative in FIFA. Furthermore, he became involved in setting up the Russian Olympic Committee. He also was coach of the Russian squad that participated in the Stockholm Olympic

October the following year, his team, the above-mentioned
St Petersburg Circle of Amateur Sportsmen[6] played a match.
This took place on the First Cadet Corps' Parade Ground on
Vasilievsky Island – surrounded by the Bolshaya Neva and
Malaya Neva rivers and the Gulf of Finland. That day, the
opposing team was the Circle of Sport Lovers – the players in
which were mainly Englishmen. The match, which ended with
the foreigners winning 6–1, is deemed to be organised Russian
football's foundational match. In early 1898, the *Peterburgsky
Kruzhok Sportsmenov* (St Petersburg Circle of Sportsmen)
was created, which on 13 September that year took on a

Games (1912). A pioneer of his country's sports journalism, Duperron
covered the Paris Olympic Games in 1900, and wrote in magazines such
as *Samokat*, *Le Cycliste* and *Sport*. He became the first referee in footballing history, in 1908, and he served as coach for the national football team. As a historian and theoretician of Russian sport, Duperron
published over thirty books on sporting matters – particularly focusing
on football, track and field, gymnastics and winter sports. He was the
promoter behind the introduction of the French gymnastics' method –
designed by Georges Demenÿ – in Bolshevik Russia. In 1921 and 1927,
he was arrested by the Soviet secret police accused of carrying out counter-revolutionary activities due to his membership of the Russian *Sokol*
Federation. In 1930, the authorities had him dismissed from the public
library he worked in, pointing to his 'bourgeois origins'. On 23 July 1934,
he died in Leningrad. It was only in 1989 that his reputation was publicly
restored. Eight years later, as part of Russian football's centenary, a me-
morial plaque was put up in honour of him and other relevant figures in
Russia's footballing history.
6   St Petersburg's Circle of Amateur Sportsmen was founded in 1888
and helped disseminate different sporting activities in Russia. In May
1897, a football section was created which – from 1902 – played in the
local league under the name Sport. It was the first team playing in the
championship that was made up of Russians. After the 1917 revolution,
the club began being called *Skoraya Pomoshch* (First Aid) until – in 1921
– the team recovered the name Sport. All the same, in 1925, its name
changed for the last time, with the club becoming known as *Petrogradsky
Rayon* until it disappeared in 1927.

'Sport' team strengthened by having included the odd British footballer.

From then on, football continued to expand, as shown by the fact that, in 1900, there were seven Russian clubs doing this sport in the city: Yekaterinhof Amateur Sports Circle, Lakhtinsky, Piotrovsky, Krestovsky, Kolomyagi Amateur Sports Circle, Staroderevo Amateur Sports Circle, and the Rossiya Circle of Footballers. These regularly played against two teams of foreigners living in the capital: Prussia (the club for settlers from Germany, linked to the German Football Federation) and the Special Circle of Sportsmen for Playing Football and Lawn Tennis of the Superior Society of the English Colony (made up of members of Britain's diplomatic corps that were stationed in the city). The matches started to be ruled according to the English game's code – appropriately translated, as we have said, by Georges A. Duperron. The Amateur Ski Sports Society (OLLS) was established the following year. This was a club restricted to members of Russia's high society and the highest-ranking officers in the Imperial Army, which, in 1911, created its own football section – becoming the forerunner to CSKA Moscow. The members of this multi-sport club could also do boxing, track and field, and speed skating.

The appearance of new teams encouraged the formation, in 1901, of the St Petersburg Football League[7] – the first competition with regular games played in Imperial Russia (as Moscow did not develop a similar tournament until 1910). Duperron was one of its founders. Indeed, he held the position

7   One of the League's first presidents was Arthur McPherson, a Scottish wood merchant who performed this role in two periods (1903–1905 and 1912–1913). He also led the Russian Football Federation (1912–1913). After the 1917 October Revolution, he was jailed and died two years later from typhoid. McPherson was a founder of the Krestovsky Lawn Tennis Club and the first president of the All-Russian Union of Lawn Tennis.

of general secretary of the body, organising the contest until 1914. The three clubs playing the first championship (*Nevka*,[8] *Nevsky*,[9] and *Victoria*) were made up of foreign residents in the city who worked in each of the local textile factories. At that time, no team had its own pitch. The competition consisted of two rounds, in each of which every team played four matches. *Nevsky* won the title with two wins, two draws, seven goals for, and four, against. As the victor, it was handed the trophy by the English businessman Thomas M. Aspden, after which the contest became known as the Aspden Cup. The competition continued to be played until 1917. In its second edition, the trophy also went to *Nevsky*, after it won all of its matches.

Usually, *Nevsky's* players would train on land next to the spinning factory of the same name. Regarding *Nevka*, the club was located in the Vyborg district. Victoria, for its part, played on the First Cadet Corps' Parade Ground on Vasilievsky Island; while the Circle of Amateur Sportsmen played on Krestovsky Island – surrounded by the Neva tributaries.[10]

---

8 Club formed in 1900 from Scots working at the Sampson weaving mill in St Petersburg. Its sporting activity came to an end in 1904. Many of the Scots coming to the country originated from towns such as Strathaven, Condorrat, Bridgeton and Calton. The repression meted out in response to the radical rising that took place following the Peterloo Massacre (1819), made many of these weavers leave the country to avoid being murdered or deported to Australia.

9 Football society founded in 1900 by English employees at the Neva Spinning Mill. The club was disbanded in 1912.

10 In the 1930s, the site housed a recreation centre for the city. Construction of a stadium began in 1934, the architect for which was Aleksandr Nikolsky, who designed a multi-sport venue with a 100,000-spectator capacity, leading the venue to be popularly known as the Nikolsky Stadium. Because of the 1941 German invasion, work on it was suspended until after the Second World War. Finally, the facilities were inaugurated on 30 July 1950 with a match that saw Zenit and Dinamo Leningrad play each other. Three decades later, the stadium was remodelled for the Moscow Olympic Games. Later, rebuilding took place

The complete control of Russian football's ruling bodies enjoyed by foreigners – in particular Brits – was perceived as an effective way of excluding locals from the sport's power structures. Tensions over such did not just surface in meetings and offices. Soon they arose in matches. In 1903, a match between Sport (the St Petersburg Circle of Amateur Sportsmen) and *Nevsky* ended with a player being sent off after attempting to throttle a player on the opposing side. The tournament administrators punished the footballer in question by giving him a year-long match ban. Sport took the decision as an affront, as its team was of homegrown players, and asked the other non-foreigner clubs to leave the competition. Resolution came, however, with the new inclusion in the tournament of two teams consisting of Russians: the *Petrovsky* and the *Nationsaly*. In 1908, a new sending off, this time of a British footballer, rekindled the controversy. A local *New Times* match report described the expulsion as a blatant infringement of football rules and breaching '[r]ules of normal civility adhered to by educated people'.[11]

The frictions between the foreigner clubs and those of homegrown Russians continued. The fact that the capital's football governing body remained in the hands of outsiders encouraged new tensions to surface. Russians questioned cases of refereeing they saw as biased towards the teams formed by Brits and Germans. They also protested against

for the third Goodwill Games – held in 1994 – and St Petersburg's 300th anniversary celebration – in 2003. Finally in 2008, the old stadium was knocked down to make way for a new venue to host the home matches for the St Petersburg club Zenit.

11   P. McConville, 'Did Scottish Weavers Teach Revolution to the Russians as well as Football?', *Random Thoughts Re Scots Law* (blog), 2012. http://scotslawthoughts.wordpress.com/2012/10/17/did-scottish-weavers-teach-revolution-to-the-russians-as-well-as-football-by-ecojon/ (last accessed 9 February 2017).

some sending offs that they felt were unwarranted, and over the varying criteria applied when penalising footballers for violent conduct. Thus, in 1903, *Sport* magazine criticised the decision by the local League Committee of banning Chirtsov – a Sport player – for one year for a hard tackle while exonerating Sharples – a British player – for punching an opponent. An angry journalist responded, '[i]n the future we shall probably have Jim the Stabber and Jack the Ripper! Match reports will be crime reports ... Let Russian clubs band together and form their own league'.[12]

All of these matters only accentuated the nationalist sentiment there was in the indigenous Russian clubs in a context shaped by the Russo–Japanese War (1904–1905, and which was followed by revolution in 1905).[13] In the military conflict, which came about due to the two countries' expansionism in Korea and Manchuria, the Japanese inflicted a humiliating defeat on its adversary. The high social and economic cost of the war urged the signing of an armistice. The relevant Treaty – Portsmouth – showed that both empires were exhausted. The consequences were immediate. Russia's failure put an end to its plans for expansion in the Far East, while the Japanese Army occupied Korea.

Because of this disaster, the Russian government chose to make some changes. The Ministries of War and Education jointly agreed to include gymnastics and track and field in the school curriculum. This was aimed at improving the physical level of the country's youth in readiness for future military conflicts. For that reason, Tsar Nicolas II appointed General

12   Riordan, *Sport in Soviet Society*, p. 24.
13   On 15 July 1904, Minister of the Interior Vyacheslav Konstantinovich Plehve was assassinated in the sixth attempt on his life. A year later, another attack, carried out by a Social Revolutionary Party member, killed the Grand Duke Sergei Alexandrovich Romanov in Moscow.

Voyeikov to be Chief Supervisor of the Physical Development of the Population of the Russian Empire – as there was still no federal structure. A committee for such was formed in 1912 with the aim of monitoring and extending these activities to encompass schools across the country, and at the same time spread state control to all Russian sports clubs.[14] Moreover, it was hoped that people's participation in pro physical-education campaigns would improve morale and domestic unity and would divert workers and students away from revolutionary activism and street hooliganism. The government's physical-education drive also encouraged a proliferation of new sports societies. Thus, the example set by the associations that emerged in the big Russian cities in the last decade of the century soon spread to the rest of the Empire – particularly after the 1905 Revolution.[15]

Times were changing. In 1904, the number of clubs made up of Russians now exceeded those of foreigners. Four years later, Sport managed to win the Aspden Cup – the first time a Russian team had won the title. That humiliation, which became a key point in football's blooming in the country, led the teams formed by foreigners to leave the 1909 tournament. They then formed their own league – calling it the Russian Society of Amateur Footballers – and organised a tournament held in 1910, the cup for which was presented by British ambassador Sir Arthur Nicholson. The other St Petersburg and Moscow teams boycotted this 'foreign league', as a result

14   By the time the First World War began, the committee Voyeikov presided over did control all of the sports organisations there were in Russia.

15   One of the main demands of the workers that participated in that unsuccessful anti-government revolt was reducing the working day – then of twelve hours. This was included in a petition that the demonstrators tried to take to the Tsar.

of which (due to a lack of participants) the settlers had to abandon the project in 1911 and return to the competitions played by the Russian clubs. Despite this rapprochement, nothing would be the same again.

The years of British and German domination were a thing of the past. Improvements to the Russians' game meant that no team made up of foreigners would win the local league again. This change was also accompanied by football spreading among the popular classes. That is how the restrictions previously imposed by the elites came to an end.

4

Industrialisation, Workers, and the Rise of Muscovite Football

Playing football had become well-established and had spread in St Petersburg among foreign settlers, and that section of the local aristocracy most favouring modernisation and standard-isation with Western Europe. Yet, in Moscow – the old Russian capital – the sport was introduced as a result of the industri-alisation process the city and its surroundings went through in the last decade of the century. Moscow became the main manufacturing centre used by British cotton-goods producers. This attracted a large contingent of skilled textile workers, which led to the forming of a colony of around 1,500 Britons, many of whom were employed as managers, carders, weavers, or engineers in textile factories in the Moscow area. Some, despite the harsh weather, decided to settle there, get married, and start a family. Most came from towns in Lancashire (such as Bolton, Darwen, or Blackburn). This was a county in which, during those years, football had risen to be the epicentre of workers' social lives as a result of Blackburn Rovers' victories: three FA Cup titles between 1884 and 1886. A three-in-a-row after twice beating Scotland's Queen's Park and in the latter year West Bromwich Albion.

In such a context, it was not odd that those English workers reached Russia wanting to emulate their idols by playing football. According to records, the first matches played in Moscow were in the 1880s, when those same Brits would run after a ball on wasteland near the city centre. As well as the outside contribution to the Russian game, there also was an attempt at spreading football by associating it with the 'Hygienist' movement. In 1896, doctors Dementyev and Pokrovsky created a team to popularise the game as a form of healthy outdoor physical exercise and thus have citizens share its benefits. Nonetheless, in spite of their efforts, football remained almost exclusively linked to British-managed factories in that decade.

Among the main promoters of the sport in the city were the brothers Clement and Henry Charnock – two ardent Blackburn Rovers fans. Both came from Chorley – a Lancashire borough – and were born in 1865 and 1870, respectively.[1] In 1887, after finishing their studies, Clement arrived in Russia and found a job as assistant manager at the Savva-Morozov-owned textile factory in Orekhovo-Zuevo (to the east of Moscow, towards the Vladimir province), one of the most notable hubs of cotton-industrial production in the nineteenth century.[2]

---

1   These two sons (out of four) of the couple William and Mary Charnock both studied at Mintholme College. This was a private school near to Preston; a city which, in that era, had one of Britain's most important football clubs: Preston North End (founded as a cricket club in 1862, and which became one of the teams that created the English football league in 1888). Later, the two gained technical education as engineering apprentices at the firm of Platt Bros. of Oldham. This was one of the biggest textile companies in the late nineteenth century and had 12,000 employees around the world. The families' links with that company would strengthen when their younger brother, Ted, married Edith – a member of the Platt family.

2   The city started producing cotton goods back in 1797. By 1890, the city had 17 factories employing over 30,000 workers. One was the weaving mill at Nikolskoye, owned by the aforementioned philanthropist and textile magnate Savva Morozov. He was an industrialist known for giving donations to revolutionary parties and Moscow's Theatre of the Arts. Yet, in 1885, the factory's 8000 workers went on strike for better working conditions – an action that pushed the authorities to introduce the first

There he decided to spread football among his workmates with the aim of creating a factory team. The Morozov family had reservations about this, but despite these were convinced by Clement to invest in the idea and provide a playing field. Charnock was able to procure a suitable working environment for his workers, who enjoyed free accommodation with hot and cold running water, had a theatre, and were even given classes in music and painting. The aim was to create a healthy workforce and improve the productivity of operatives who, being mainly illiterate and from rural areas, were unused to factory discipline. To achieve these goals, Clement Charnock encouraged them to do sports in their spare time. His main idea was none other than to get them away from their main recreational habit on Sundays – the one free day of the week.[3] This was excessive vodka drinking, which would lead to serious work absenteeism on Mondays.[4] Moreover, it was hoped that football would have the knock-on effect of providing social peace in the family's factories. This was after they had suffered several industrial disputes, such as the 1885 and 1890 strikes that had degenerated into violent disturbances.

Charnock's first attempt was not so successful; after inflating, in front of his workers, a ball he had brought from England, Charnock kicked it powerfully into the air, causing the ball to

measures benefiting labour in Russia. The first Charnock to work in the company was James who was the factory's first technical manager and earned 20,000 roubles a year. Clement and Harry worked as employees in the spinning factory built in 1805, by Maxim Konshin, in Serpukhov – an urban area to the south of Moscow.

3   Although a law, passed on 2 June 1897, limited the working day to eleven and a half hours (ten for Saturdays and the days before public holidays), often employers forced their staff to work 13 or 14 hours a day, six days a week.

4   Despite this intention, it was common for, at half time, players to go to the side to regain strength by drinking lemon juice, lemonade, or beer.

land with a loud bang. Then, the Brit watched in dismay as his frightened workers fled from it. But Clement was not to be put off. He ordered a pitch to be levelled and marked out, and for poles to be erected to simulate goals. Additionally, he handed out to those workers willing to play, blue and white football kits (precisely blue shirts with white collars and cuffs, white pants and black socks). These he himself had ordered from his country and were in honour of his beloved Blackburn Rovers. The budget he had, however, did not go far enough to buy boots for the players, which were too expensive. So, the participants had to play in their own shoes.[5]

All the same, the limited enthusiasm shown by the workers led to a loss of heart for the oldest of the Charnock brothers, who, within a year, gave up on the initial idea of creating a factory football team. Although he did try picking up the project again, he left the factory to become the director at another in Sereda (a town 60 kilometres to the south of Moscow), owned by the Gorbunnofs family. This led him to put the idea on hold.

Like his older brother, Henry was an avid fan of both football and, of course, 'the Riversiders' (Blackburn Rovers). After finishing his academic education, he went off to India and Central Asia to gain first-hand knowledge of trading. With all that experience behind him, in 1893, he went to Russia to be deputy manager of the Morozov factory in Orek-hovo-Zuevo, of which his uncle, James Charnock, was head director. He soon resurrected his brother's idea of setting up a factory team. To avoid the idea coming to nothing, Henry saw the need to involve fellow countrymen in the team that could provide footballing experience. With this in mind, he

5   A pair of boots made by The Scrum – the most reputable brand in those years – would cost five roubles.

published adverts in the *London Times* and the *Daily Telegraph* in which jobs were offered to engineers, mechanics, and clerks capable of 'playing football well'. The offer even attracted a professional player from Bolton Wanderers. But there was still an obstacle to overcome: the aversion to the existence of workers' sports clubs by Tsarist authorities who did not approve of independent workers' organisations (which were taken to be seditious and revolutionary threats). In order for clubs to begin their activity, they needed official permits issued by the provincial governor that made clear that they didn't represent any danger.

But the authorities were not the only ones who did not sympathise with the idea of workers playing football. The Orthodox Church's most conservative sect, known as the 'Old Believers' (*raskolniki*), did not see the sporting activity as appropriate either. In that era, people tended to be extremely conservative and, resultingly, inclined towards these Christians' narrow ethos. Any intrusion of a 'German' nature – to use the word applied to all foreigners in Russia in those years – aroused suspicion, however small this influence might be (as was the case with football). For that reason, when a young man started playing soccer, he would come across a lot of resistance from his parents. The Old Believers, who also were in favour of prohibiting alcohol and tobacco consumption, would force players to wear trousers to avoid showing naked knees as they considered exposing one's body to be immoral.[6] It is no surprise, therefore, that some players turned

---

6   Despite these initial reservations, by 1910, the first teams linked to the Russian Church were being created. These included *Rogozhskaya*, which in 1911 was playing in the Muscovite second division, and a team from Moscow's theological seminar. Talented people came out of these teams, such as Sergei Krasovsky, a centre-forward who played at the St Vladimir seminary between 1911 and 1913. Years later, he would be-

up at matches with shorts reaching their ankles. In the middle of a match, tired of discomfort, Henry Charnock cut down the trousers he was wearing with a pair of scissors.

Despite the Englander being ignorant of any ill will towards his project, the truth is that the company owners – the Morozov family – were close to the Old Believers[7] and did not approve of their employees spending their breaktime playing a game they considered to be sinful. Paradoxically this rejection was related to football being equated with modernity. And it was precisely for that same reason that a section of well-off young Russians began to play it, seeing it to be the best way to be associated with the most modern and industrialised societies. In order to appear like the Brits and Germans and that kicked balls about, the Muscovites copied them – from their kit through to their language. In no time, football became the most popular sport in the city, with over a thousand players and a growing number of spectators.

Meanwhile, Henry Charnock, determined to overcome the administrative obstacles that prevented registering the club officially, travelled to Vladimir – the provincial capital – to meet with the governor. During the meeting, the top authority in the province felt overwhelmed by the extravagant Briton who zealously talked to him about a sporting activity he did not understand. He asked, '[w]hat is football?' Patiently, the young Charnock responded: 'A game played by 22 players, divided equally, to obtain possession of an inflated rubber

come a soloist at the Bolshoi Theatre.

7   The Morozov came from the village of Zuevo, located 85 kilometres to the east of Moscow. It was there that the patriarch of this merchant family was born: Savva Vasilyevich – a peasant turned owner of two craft workshops (Zuev and Nikolskoye). In 1820 he moved to Moscow, the moment when he took the surname Morozov – referring to the harsh winter that characterised the month, February, in which he was born. His rural origin explains his link with the Old Believers.

and leather sphere, and each trying to drive it through posts fixed at the ends of a playing field'. Once the description was heard, the local head denied the request after stating, 'And people meet to watch that? What stupidity!'[8] Instead of acquiescing, Charnock played his trump card: showing the man a photograph of the Crown Prince of the German Empire, Wilhelm of Prussia, playing football with his officer teammates on a pitch in Tempelhof (Berlin).[9] Moreover, the Brit did not hesitate to add, 'as you well know, His Excellency is the cousin of our gracious ruler the Tsar'.[10] The reminder worked and finally the team could be constituted under the name Orekhovo Sports Club (KSO) – although receiving definitive formal approval still took some years. Charnok was made club president; Kupriyanov, vice-chair; and Bodrov, secretary.

At first, the club was only allowed to register employees – of either sex – at the Morozov factory. As well as football, KSO's 250 full members could play other sports, such as tennis, cricket, cycling, ice skating, and track and field.

---

8   D. Downing, *Passovotchka. Moscow Dynamo in Britain, 1945* (London: Bloomsbury Publishing, 1999), p. 70.

9   The last Crown Prince of the Kingdom of Prussia and the German Empire, and member of the Hohenzollern Dynasty, was a sports lover. His favourite sports were football and tennis. In 1908, he gave a cup to the German Football Federation, which led to the creation of a competition called the *Kronprinzenpokal* (Crown Prince Cup) – the oldest tournament in German football. In the first championship held, it was the different regional associations that played each other, and victory went to the pick from *Mitteldeutschland* (Central Germany), which beat the Berlin team 1–3 in the final. The tournament was played from 1908 to 1919, after which its name changed to the *Bundespokal* (Federal Cup).

10   At that point, the governor's wife interrupted the conversation to suggest that her husband try playing the English game. Thinking over the proposal, the governor responded that he 'greatly admired the English even if they did beat their wives'. Downing, *Passovotchka*, p. 70.

5

Morozovtsy – the First Great Team

At first, the Orekhovo Sports Club (KSO) consisted of the factory's British engineers and managers, such as Heywood, Dunkerley, Bertel, Tomlinson, and the Charnock brothers. They were joined, among others, by young Russians like Nikolay Makarov; the brothers Vladimir and Anatoli Mixin; the other siblings Aleksandr and Nikolay Kinin; Peter Chichvarykyn; Mikhail Savintsev; and Aleksandr Kononov. These members of the '*Morozovitsy*', as the team became popularly known, began training on a field next to the Hopper factory.[1] Soon, Muscovites became interested in this peculiar game in which participants chased a ball bouncing around. Training matches would get to attract around 300 curious onlookers.

Henry Charnock's example was soon emulated by other managers who created football teams in their own factories, as was the case with Mercury, which regularly included well-to-do citizens and foreign residents. This explains how football got to spread beyond Moscow's boundaries. These 'sportsmen's' high purchasing power allowed them to have *dachas* (country holiday homes), normally in adjoining areas, where they spent seasonal or bank holidays. They would use their leisure time to play football: thereby publicising the sport among the local population. All of this facilitated spreading the sport to the Muscovite suburbs, as well as those towns

1   Some sources even claim that the employees of this factory were the first to play a football game in Moscow – taking place in 1895.

and villages located along the railway lines from Moscow. The expectations aroused by its propagation were considerable, to the extent that a Russian journalist, D. Blagoev, did not hesitate in affirming, '[s]occer has become the most interesting thing to watch in Moscow'.[2]

In autumn 1905, there was a meeting between some of the city's football's pioneers: such as both the Filippov and Charnock brothers, Fyodor Rozanov, Vladimir Vinogradov, and Mikhail Dubinin. Their aim was to publicise the sport in Moscow and encourage setting up new clubs. Indeed, because of the 1905 revolutionary upsurge, many employers had decided to create teams to keep their staff away from political activity. By the following year, Morozov had built a sports club at his factory in Orekhovo-Zuevo.[3]

To contribute to the spread of football, a match managed to be arranged between two mixed teams representing Moscow and St Petersburg. Thousands of spectators attended it on 14 September 1907. The away team, which ended up winning 0–2, included some Britons in its line-up that day. The draw was repeated for a while and almost always the St Petersburg team was the one securing victory. The inter-city match, on top of creating a rivalry between the two most important urban conurbations in the country, was crucial to Russian football's development. It also made visible two different conceptions of the game: the Muscovite model based on a vigorous long-passing game – as was characteristic in British football, and the

---

2 P. A. Frykholm, 'Soccer and Social Identity in Pre-Revolutionary Moscow', *Journal of Sport History*, vol. 24, no. 2, summer 1997, p. 144.

3 His example was followed, in 1912, by the Putilov plant management, who agreed to set up the Circle of Amateur Sportsmen. Likewise, Welsh industrialist Ivor Hughes sponsored football clubs at each of his steel factories in Iuzovka. Workers' teams were also established in the cities of Kharkiv and Kramatorsk in eastern Ukraine, among others.

short-passing game based on possession that was standard in the capital's teams.

From 1906, new Moscow clubs – most of which were multi-sport – were created, such as 'Union' (founded in the north of the city in 1908, made up of Germans, and sponsored by the employer Chokolov); the British Sports Club (BSC); Rogozhsky Sports Circle (RKS); and Zamoskvoretsky Sports Circle (ZKS, founded in April 1910). Teams from Moscow's surroundings would also emerge, in areas such as Mamontovka, Izmaylovo, Rastorguevo, or Petrovsky Park. Most of the teams took the name of the factory or borough they represented, or even that of the closest railway station. Like the aforementioned Mercury, others adopted names that would impress their rivals. Their members, as well as foreign managers and engineers, were well-to-do urban merchants or industrialists who had the luxury of being able to pay the membership fees. For patrons, presiding over clubs, far from bringing them financial rewards, was a way to increase their social prestige and political influence.

This proliferation aided – on the initiative of 'the sportsman' Robert Ferdinandovich Fulda[4] (founder of *Sokolnichesky*

---

4   Born in 1873 into a family of German merchants that had emigrated to Russia in the second half of the nineteenth century. His father, Ferdinand Fulda, had been awarded the title of Hereditary Honorary Citizen of Russia. Robert graduated in law from Moscow University. He became interested in sport, particularly football and tennis, becoming one of the pioneers of Russian football. In 1904, he translated from English the Football Association rules and organised the Muscovite football league. The year after, he co-founded the *Sokolnichesky Klub Sporta* (Sokolniki Sports Club). In 1912, he was a technical assistant for the Russian national team that participated in the Stockholm games. Two years later, he took up the post of national-team manager. He was president of Moscow's Olympic Committee between 1912 and 1920 and of the Russian Football Union from 1914 to 1918. After the outbreak of the October Revolution in 1917, Fulda fled the country. After briefly living in Germany, he ended up settling in Switzerland, where he died in 1944.

Klub Sporta, SKS) – the establishment of the first official Muscovite football league. The League's founding constitution was overseen and approved by the mayor of Moscow on 21 December 1909. The foundational assembly for the championship was held in the summer of 1910.[5] Although only four clubs participated in the first season,[6] by 1913 the tournament had 25 teams split into three groupings. Teams included the previously mentioned SKS (the first consisting only of homegrown Russians, founded in 1905),[7] *Kruzhok Futbolistov Sokolniki* (KFS), and the *Moskovsky Klub Lyzhnikov* (MKL), and there was also a refereeing team. The size of football's expansion was additionally shown by the incorporation of women into playing the game. In 1911, Russian women's football began its journey, and Moscow was the first city where it took place. Among its pioneers were students from the Kirpichnikova school and those that studied at business schools and colleges. The first female soccer game played in the city was held on 13 August that year. The opposing teams were Pushkin and Petrovsko-Razumovskaya. Under heavy rain, the Pushkin players managed to beat their rivals by a hefty 5–0,

---

5   On 2 June 1910, an inaugural dinner for that first Moscow football season was held at the Hermitage restaurant – then, one of the most famous in the city.
6   The four teams that participated in the city's first league season were Union, Sokolniki Sports Club (SKS), Orekhovo Sports Club (KSO), and the British Sports Club (BSC). That year, the winning team was given a trophy that had been donated by Roman Fulda.
7   That year, the *Sokolniki*, as they were popularly known, built their own stadium. This was a fenced-off area that had benches as makeshift stands to accommodate the public. It was Moscow's first football ground. In 1908, the club acquired a pavilion so that its members could train during the winter. The next year, the club's heads decided to render tribute to one of its founders; the German-origin jewellery magnate, Robert Ferdinandovich Fulda, by naming the stadium after him.

with Jurina scoring four. Soon, similar teams would be formed in Presnya and Semenov.

Without a doubt, KSO was the master of Russian football in those years. It is no coincidence that it was popularly known as the 'Moscow storm'. Between 1910 and 1914, the team promoted by Charnock managed to win five Moscow League championships in a row, as well as the first Fulda Cup (1910). This was with a team made up of Russians and Brits, among which were three members of the Charnock family (Ted and Billy – Henry's younger brothers and who worked in Ser-pukhov's Konshin factory – and their cousin Jimmy), British Army captain Archibald Wavell,[8] and Robert Hill Bruce Lockhart – a Scottish diplomat who played as forward from 1912.[9] The team's various successes meant that its matches would bring over 10,000 spectators, of which 30 per cent were women. According to Lockhart, the team tried to emulate the

8   In 1911, Wavell spent a year as a military observer in the Russian army. He combined his military duties with playing matches for the KSO team. After his short stay in Russia, Wavell fought in the First World War and was wounded in the eye in the Battle of Ypres. Once recovered, in 1916, he was posted to Turkey as liaison officer with the Russian army. Two years later, he became attached to the British High Command in Palestine.

9   Journalist and writer, Lockhart joined the British Ministry of For-eign Affairs and was seconded to Moscow to be Vice-Consul. In 1912, he joined the Morozov factory football team, which managed to win the local championship (for which the gold medal he was given is now part of the National Library of Scotland collection). After the 1917 Bolshevik revolution, he had to leave the country, although he returned as a Brit-ish diplomatic envoy in January 1918. That same year, he was arrested alongside the intelligence agent Sidney Reilly for participating in a plot to assassinate Lenin. Lockhart was condemned to death but, before he could be executed, was exchanged with Russian diplomat Maxim Litvin-ov, who had been arrested in Britain. In 1932, his autobiographical work *Memoirs of a British Agent* saw the light of day. For the above information we have consulted the 2011 Frontline Books edition.

old Newcastle United playing system and the Scottish style based on controlling the ball and dribbling with it.

In October 1910, the year in which the company eventually decided to build a comfortable 10,000-seater ground, KSO played its first 'international' fixture. Its rival was Sport Club Corinthians – the name Slavia Prague gave itself on its trips abroad. The match ended with a home win thanks to a goal by Newman. That day, around 5000 spectators gathered at the stadium, wanting to see the Czech aces in action. Indeed, expectations ran so high that they even sold tickets in advance. After a mini-tour by KSO, in which it played three matches in St Petersburg, the Moscow team's players began to wear striped shirts like those worn by its opponents. In this regard, Yuri Korchak, one of KSO's homegrown players, reminisced, '[w]e wanted to be like the famous foreigners'.[10] The following year, Moscow was toured by a German team, *Berlin*, who played three matches against its hosts: of which two ended in victories for the away team. Meanwhile, The Wanderers, a team of English football players, came to St Petersburg to play three games – one day after another. They won all three: defeating a team bringing together both local and Moscow players, a selection of national players, and then a team made up of Englanders living in the city. The press had no hesitation in acknowledging the talent of the local teams' opponents: '[w]e lost these international matches, but, after all, we were playing against the founders of the game, against our teachers'.[11]

By the end of the decade, football's popularisation had become absolutely clear. Around the game, business was budding. Matches were announced using posters placed on newsstands, and on walls and trams. Some of the biggest

---

10   P. A. Frykholm, 'Soccer and Social Identity in Pre-Revolutionary Moscow', pp. 143–154.

11   Riordan, *Sport in Soviet Society*, p. 28.

department stores in Moscow, such as the Muir and Mirrielees or the first specialised sports shops, such as *Vse dlia Sporta* (Everything for Sport) located on the Bolshaya Nikitskaya, began to sell footballs, kits, and boots.

New clubs were incorporated into the league, including Malakhova and Sheremetyevo. Contributing to this growth was coverage of matches in the new sports press. Chronicles praised the benefits brought by football:

> [a] sport that requires healthy lungs and hearts … The healthy people participating in it do not just improve their health, but they develop all of their bodily organs and muscles … Football is unimaginable without there being encouragement and courage … it unconsciously instils a feeling of brotherhood among all participants in the game. It is one of the cheapest and most accessible sports. Yes, often there are accidents but soccer is not responsible for the inexperience and lack of care of young players … with the right training the risk of accidents in a game in reduced to a minimum.[12]

It is, consequently, no surprise that clubs were set up everywhere, even though some encountered obstacles, such as the impossibility of finding a suitable playing surface on which to play football. They overcame these impediments as best as they could. Railway workers, for instance, went as far as improvising matches on the tracks, despite the authorities banning this activity. Meanwhile, some of those running clubs began to offer financial rewards to sign up the best talent. Thus, *Union* paid a sum of five roubles, while Zamoskvoretsky Sports Club offered three roubles and five kopeks. The pioneer

---

12 Text taken from https://www.bogorodsk-noginsk.ru/socium/21_futbol.html (Last accessed: 12 February 2022).

of this practice was *Sokolniki*, who, from July 1910, awarded their players five roubles. These were payments generally compensated by the profits obtained from ticket sales. In those years, in which advance sales rarely took place, adults would pay 40 cents to enter a stadium, while students only had to pay half that.

Likewise, the arrival of winter prevented football from being played at a time in which covered stadiums did not yet exist. The low temperatures, which affected the playing fields, made it impracticable to play sports outdoors. For that reason, when the football activity ceased, most players switched to playing ice hockey – the version known as Russian *bandy*. For that reason, it was common for footballers to have a long list of achievements – due to trophies they won in *both* hockey and football.

The Tsarist authorities disliked the proliferation of workers' teams, being wary about the degree of self-organisation showed when workers created their own clubs. They also were unhappy about the multitudes – sometimes noisy – that gathered outside stadiums. For those reasons, the Moscow police went as far as breaking up worker teams, fearful that they served to harbour subversive political activities within them. Football began to attract a lot of people and the security forces believed that it was used to mask revolutionary agitation. The authorities would go as far as suggesting that some workers took advantage of it to carry out armed military exercises. This attitude is hardly surprising if we take into account that it was precisely in the Morozov family's factories where some of the most militant strikes took place. Indeed, the authorities' fears were not baseless. Workers at St Petersburg's Obukhov metallurgical plant – created in 1863 and specialised in producing naval-artillery equipment – tended to meet in secluded areas on the banks of the Neva River to train themselves at using hand grenades and the like, as well as to practice fighting, fencing and military techniques. Other examples include the factories in Kharkiv, Moscow, Oryol, and Ivanovo-Voznesensk, or the members of the Rostov Workers' Boxing Club – founded in 1905 – who combined hand-gun shooting with studying the works of Karl Marx.

But nor did left-wing and trade-union organisations approve of football's lure on workers. They harshly criticised the creation of factory teams, believing that they undermined endeavours to unionise and radicalise workers. Football was perceived as a deviant activity: a distraction that stopped the working class from developing political consciousness.

Despite these reproaches and the attempts to draw labour away from football, worker's interest in the sport grew continually, particularly in the big cities, where any space – fields, meadows, courtyards, parks, and particularly cemeteries – was good for a game. Rather than managing to shrink its appeal at all, soccer became the quintessential working-class sport – as had occurred in Britain. The masses now packing out the stadiums demonstrated that the authorities' manoeuvres had been in vain. Overtaken by events, in the end the rulers had no choice but to give in. This helped the first official league of workers' clubs to be set up – in 1911.

In this period, the first footballer idols emerged. An example was the left-winger Vasily Zhitarev, who Moscow's *Zamoskvoretsky Klub Sporta* (ZKS) signed in 1911 from *Kruzhok Futbolistov Sokolniki* (KFS), and who ended up as a big celebrity in Russia.

PART II

Boyhood

Отрочество

6

The Newly Created Russian Football Union and the Stockholm Games

Football's popularisation was not a process devoid of tension. When Russian workers wanted to join the country's most distinguished football clubs, they were blocked from doing so by the organisations' foreign members. These came from better-off backgrounds and had no intention of socialising with the workers. This rejection produced an increase in anti-British sentiment and the first conflicts. In the process of appropriating football, Russians gave the sport undertones of a national and – at the beginning – class character. And any milestones achieved while playing an imported sport were to boost pride in the nation.

In order to avoid new incidents, regularise the game's playing, and bring together the country's football clubs, on 19 January 1912, the Russian Football Union (RFS) was created.[1] This was the materialisation of an idea envisaged two years earlier, when the St Petersburg Football League proposed

1   The constituent assembly for the RFS was held at the Vienna restaurant in Moscow – on the corner of the Malaya Morskaya and Gorokhovaya Streets. Those attending chose Arthur D. McPherson to be the first chairman of the federal body. The deputy chairmanships went to both Ferdinandovich Fulda (who would be President from 1914 to 1915) and Hartley. The post of secretary was taken by Duperron, and treasurer by Shints. Also on the governing board were Baines, Pearson, and Shultz.

creating a single administration. In the preparatory meetings to formalise the foundations for this, club representatives from three cities attended: C. G. Bertram and R. F. Fulda for Moscow;[2] A. D. McPherson, G. Hartley, and Georges A. Duperron for St Petersburg; and S. P. Nesterov on behalf of Sevastopol.

With its headquarters being in Moscow, the association, which joined FIFA on 30 June that year, was made responsible for watching over compliance with footballing rules, as well as organising League and Cup tournaments. At first, the body included 52 clubs from St Petersburg, Moscow, Odessa,[3] Riga, Kiev, Kharkiv,[4] and the Polish Łódź. In less than a year, it had affiliated to it 155 societies from 33 different cities, covering a total of 4000 players.

Its members reached an agreement on not playing more than three British players per team and on recognising the FIFA-approved rules of the game. Despite this, the new organisation did not allow the inclusion of worker clubs, given that they were not deemed to be 'true amateurs'. A few years later, the ban was lifted – coinciding with the outbreak of the First World War.

The Federation also laid the foundations for the Russian national team, which from 1912 to 1914 would get to play 14 international matches. In fact, the team was speedily put together to be able to represent the country in the Stockholm Olympic Games in 1912. This was a contest in which the major

2   In 1904, Fulda wrote and distributed the first set of footballing rules in the country.

3   In spite of football reaching Odessa in the 1870s – thanks to it being a key port city, the local league there was not set in motion until 1911.

4   Both in Kharkiv and Kiev – then, the two most important cities in Ukraine – the local leagues did not start operating until 1912. But this, then, acted as a spur for universities and colleges to set up their own teams.

industrialised states – Germany, Britain, and the United States – compared their respective potential and degree of modernity through sport. Actually, Russia had already taken part in re-inventing the Olympic movement as a first-time participant in the 1908 London Olympic Games. Its five-member delegation then had to pay out of its own pocket for its trip to and stay in the British capital.

Returning to the Swedish Games, on 13 February 1912, Russian football's new governing body sent representatives to a national Olympic Committee meeting. The gathering was to decide how many competitors would represent the Empire in Stockholm. Finally, 225 were chosen, including players in the national football team.

Yet the under-representation of Muscovite sportspersons in the Olympic delegation raised tempers to the point that the Moscow clubs went as far as threatening a boycott if a balanced selection was not guaranteed. In the end, the dispute between St Petersburg and Moscow was channelled into a football match between their respective teams. The result – a 2–2 draw – did not help to lower the tension.

To be selected for the Russian team at the Games, the RFS decided that only players in Moscow or St Petersburg clubs would be eligible, a step that demonstrated the poor level of the other teams in existence. In order to prepare for the Olympic tournament, those footballers called up played several friendlies before travelling to the Swedish capital. The preparatory tour was disappointing, with an adverse goal balance: 20 against and only four goals scored.

The picking of the Russian national squad to participate in the Olympics took place in St Petersburg on 13 and 14 May. The matches that had been played then ended up determining who would be in the Russian delegation. In the middle of everything, the football heads unanimously chose to exclude one of the candidates because he had arrived late for a preparatory game.

In the end, on 12 June 1912, the Russian Olympic squad set sail from the port of St Petersburg in the 'Burma' cargo ship *en route* to Stockholm. All of its members wore straw hats adorned with the colours of the national flag. Unlike some of their colleagues in the delegation, the footballers were clear that they would not be competing for medals. 'The aim of our trip is to learn, just learn. We shouldn't be scared of losing', stated one of the young Russian footballers who went.[5]

The Olympic football tournament was played by eleven national teams. On 30 June, the Russians played their first match of the competition, and the first outside their country, against Finland. The venue was Stockholm's Tranebergs Idrottsplat stadium, which opened the previous year and was Djurgardens IF Fotboll's home ground. That day the Russian team wore yellow shirts with the national shield on the chest, and dark-blue pants. Although the Finns had played Italy the previous evening, and might have been tired, they managed to spoil the official Russian debut, beating them 2–1. A mistake by the Russian goalkeeper (Tabor taken advantage of by Wiberg), in the 30th minute opened the door to victory for the Finns. Despite St Petersburg's *Unitas*[6] forward Vasily

<hr />

5 Text taken from https://www.bogorodsk-noginsk.ru/socium/21_ futbol.html (last accessed: 15 February 2022).

6 A club based in the area of Udelnaya founded in 1911 after the merging of two teams, as promoted by Kirill Pavlovich Butusov – one of the big names associated with the organisation. It is no coincidence that as many as five of his brothers – Aleksandr, Vasily, Konstantin, Pavel, and Mikhail – also played a notable role at the club. *Unitas* was one of St Petersburg's strongest teams in the early twentieth century, which was partly thanks to including – from 1911 to 1917 – the internationally capped defender Pyotr Sokolov. Its team played in red and white. *Unitas*

Pavlovich Butusov (that day, Russian captain)[7] managing an equaliser in the 72nd minute, just eight minutes later, Jarl ('*Lali*') Öhman scored the winner for Finland.

At the time, the Great Duchy of Finland was one of the territories in the Russian Empire, after being annexed in September 1809. This resulted from the signing of the Treaty of Fredrikshamn, which ended the Finnish War (1808–1809) in which Sweden and Russia fought each other. The very same year that the Stockholm Games were held, a Law of Equality was passed, which gave Russians living in Finland the same rights as the homegrown population. This thereby culminated in the process of Russification that had begun in 1908. Adding to this controversy was the decision by the Swedish organisers of the Games to allow the Finns to compete and parade with their own flag, which hugely upset the Russians. Russian outrage grew when, on top of this, they found out that Finland would be Russia's first opponent in the Olympic football tournament. This was a real slap in the face. For all this, it is easy to imagine what it meant for the Russians to be ousted

played in the St Petersburg championship between 1911 and 1923 – the year that it was refounded under the name *Spartakus* due to the impact of the Bolshevik Revolution. It also became linked with the port town of Vyborg – located to the capital's north east and close to the Finnish border. In 1927, the club would change its name again to become *Pischevkus* (until 1930).

7   Vasily Butusov fought in the Great War in the Tsarist army until he was captured in the eastern European region of Galicia by the Germans. In October 1930, he was arrested for his alleged involvement in the 'industrial party' case. After a year in prison, he was released as a result of mediation by his brother Mikhail – then one of the USSR's football stars. He fought, years later, in the Second World War, this time as a Red Army officer on the Caucasian front. Captured in 1941, he spent four years in a concentration camp until he was freed by North American troops. When the conflict ended, he went back to playing football, together with his younger brother. When he finally hung up his boots, he went on to referee.

from the tournament by Finland: a defeat with a marked symbolic and political backdrop that hurt their national pride.

The day after, Russia took on Germany in a playoff. As opposed to this soothing any hurt, the match, which was played in front of 2000 spectators at the Råsunda Stadium in Solna, exposed the Russian team's shortcomings, as it was humiliatingly thrashed 7–0. In all, the national team's Olympic experience was pretty painful. Some commentators, after watching the team's game, did not hold back in their criticism. One wrote, 'when it comes to football, we are still children'.[8] The size of the failure produced frustration and a feeling of national inferiority. This was shown by the use of the expression 'sporting Tsushima', which compared the national team's failure to the much-remembered naval battle heralding the Russian Empire's definitive defeat by Japan during the Russo–Japanese War (1904–1905). Out of the eleven national squads participating in the Olympic football competition, Russia came ninth.

---

8   Text taken from https://www.sportsdaily.ru/articles/groza-vratarey-mihail-butusov-37543 (last accessed: 15 February 2022).

7

The First National League Championship

In March 1912, KSO travelled to Kharkiv to play two friendly matches, as was approved by the Moscow Football League. Its arrival at the Nova Bavariya train station was met with much commotion. The Muscovite team's presence in the Ukrainian city had aroused great expectations. Soon after, the League Championship would begin. And, shortly, the two best teams in the tournament – Moscow's *Morozovtsy* and St Petersburg's *Merkur* – would play each other. When that match took place, on 5 May 1912, the players that stood out from among the Muscovite home team were Charnock, Tomlinson, and Deakin.

That summer, the League Committee in Moscow decided that to raise the level of the national team, it needed to play more international matches. With that aim in mind, a game was arranged against the Hungarian Olympic team, which ended in their beating the Russians 9–0. Another disappointment for the Russian team. This inspired the establishment, in the autumn of 1912, of a national tournament with teams from St Petersburg, Moscow, Kharkiv, Riga, Kursk, Odessa, Kiev, and Yelets. Even so, the clubs that dominated Russian football remained the Muscovite and St Petersburg teams. It was no surprise that it was representatives from both cities that played in the championship final that year. The first winner of the Russian league was St Petersburg, which overcame its rival

4–2. Yet the defeat for Moscow's *Morozovtsy* was unevenly accepted. While its players acknowledged the strengths of their adversaries and 'reacted like gentlemen', the Muscovite supporters 'behaved like savages'.[1]

At the end of September 1912, Moscow was visited by a German team: Holstein Kiel, which had been founded in 1900 by members of the *Kieler Männerturnvereins von 1844* club. The outsiders prevailed by 6–0, 10–1, and 3–0 in the three games they played against *Morozovtsy* and a select Muscovite team, which proved the strength of the Germans' game. The distress caused to the Moscow club by the defeats at the hands of foreign teams was overcome through victories in local tournaments. Yet, in 1912, it was KSO that was the master of Russian football after winning the League and – for the third time in a row – the Cup. Its line-up was the most common one in that era: five up front, three in midfield, and two in defence. A 5–3–2 formation showing the offensive character of Russian football at the time.

In 1913, the following year, *Sokolniki* disappeared – due to financial problems affecting its related company. The year was also one of changes for *Morozovtsy*, as the club would be joined by new players – known as the 'second generation'. These included McDonald, Tzolkin, Krotov, Stepanov, Golubkov, Volkov, Kulikov, Andreev, and Paur. On 21 April that year, the Swedish national team visited Moscow for a friendly. Even though the Russians' playing level had improved, the match ended with another home defeat, by 1–4, before 5000 spectators. In those days, it was common for national teams to do tours. Thus, that summer, the Norwegian team came to Russia, playing three matches at the end of August. In the

---

1   Text taken from https://www.sportsdaily.ru/articles/groza-vratarey-mihail-butusov-37543 (last accessed: 15 February 2022).

first – played on 25 August – they took on *Morozovtsy*. That day, the Muscovites managed their first win in an international game. Four days later, the Norwegians won 4–1 against *Union* – Moscow's second-strongest team. Finally, they played a Russian national team that could only include local footballers, as St Petersburg did not send any. The match – played on 1 September and watched by over 8000 spectators – ended in a 1–1 draw.

These tours, as well as the visit by English coach Arthur Gaskell – a former Bolton Wanderers player, invited to come by one of the Charnock brothers – helped to develop and improve Russian footballing standards. In November 1913, there were 1,266 sports clubs in the country, 700 of which were for football, and most were located in St Petersburg or Moscow (although there was a notable amount also in Ukraine and Belorussia).[2] The increase in the number of teams led to new leagues being created in cities such as Kiev and Kharkiv. That year, the national champion was the Odessa team, but the federal governors reprimanded the Black Sea club for having included four English footballers in its line-up – when the rules only allowed three foreigners per team.

Meanwhile, in Moscow, *Morozovtsy* remained indomitable. They triumphed in the local tournament after winning eleven of twelve matches and with an enviable goals record: 44 for and only 15 against. As if that were not enough, the team picked up the Fulda Cup for the fourth consecutive year. This era of success coincided with the increasing appearance in the

2   In Ukraine there were 196 clubs with 8000 members, while in Belorussia the number of associates in sports societies – such as *Sanitas*, *Sokol*, *Bogatyr*, or *Maccabee* – reached a thousand. The latter club – linked to the Jewish Federation of Gymnastics and Sports Associations – was tolerated by Tsarism due to its aim of avoiding Jews' involvement in revolutionary political organisations.

team of homegrown Russians at the expense of the Brits. As a result, while from 1901 to 1912 the club had five English footballers, in 1913, this was reduced to three or four. A year later only two were members; and by the following year, only one representative was left in the starting line-up.

In that era, it started being commonplace that footballers changed team – something unthinkable previously. This 'lack of loyalty' came in for harsh criticism by the sporting press: stating, '[i]t is no great honour for a club to buy a player'.[3] In order to attract the best talent, the clubs would offer players everything from changing-room towels to having masseurs available, and being trained by skilled coaching staff in special facilities.

---

3 J. Riordan, *Sport in Soviet Society. Development of Sport and Physical Education in Russia and the USSR* (Cambridge: Cambridge University Press, 1977), p. 34.

8

'Wild Football' – Clandestinity, Sport, and Activism

The spread of football also brought with it the rise of the so-called 'wild' or 'outlaw' (*dikiy*) football – a popular version of the sport. This was driven by the 'social apartheid' that workers suffered by being excluded from football clubs and competitions due to their social background.

In 1910, the first teams of workers and high-school students started being set up. In Moscow, many of them used the esplanade by the Kalitnikovskoye cemetery for a kickabout. A long way from the 'sportsmen's' clubs and those with employer sponsors, these unofficial societies were treated with suspicion by the authorities. Believed to possibly harbour illegal activities, many were closed by the police.[1] This kind of intervention made people in these organisations seek other clubs where they could continue playing.

Obviously, the Russian Football Union did not recognise these teams, which it treated with contempt and arrogance. 'A team of workers playing against our clubs'? It was something unthinkable for footballing heads in that period. In fact, to

---

1   A similar thing had happened in the nineteenth century when the Imperial authorities decided to extend the banning of boxing contests (a prohibition that stayed in place until 1894). The spur was fear of the effects these could have on their extremely poor audiences. In 1832, Tsar Nicholas I decreed prohibition of bare-knuckle fights due to the concern they aroused among rural landowners, who saw how peasants could use such to train themselves to fight against their masters.

avoid them joining the tournaments, the financial contributions required to become league teams were increased, and an order was issued preventing league referees from doing 'wild team' matches. But there were 35 of these 'underground' teams just in Moscow. It was the case that football was a reflection of the growth the city was experiencing due to the rural exodus taking place in a country in the process of industrialisation.[2] But this breakneck growth was also synonymous with precariousness, extreme poverty, inadequate housing, crime, disorder, and different diseases.[3]

Yet from 1916, the situation changed and the presence of the underground teams began to be tolerated. Thus, it was common for matches to be played by teams such as the Presnensky Sports Circle, the Kremlin Circle, the Simonovsky, the Askold, and others. Prior to this, the government had chosen to accept the creation of new clubs in factories and the Imperial Army and Navy, aiming to neutralise the growing popularity of both these 'outlaw' clubs and the most militant workers. But *dikiy* football was not synonymous with workers' football as also participating in these spontaneous matches were students, public servants, employees, and 'white-collar' workers (*sluzhashchie*).

In Moscow, one of underground football's idols was Boris Chesnokov. Son of a railway worker, the small-of-stature Chesnokov made friends with several professional fighters who combined doing sport with occasional work in circuses.

---

2   In the first decade of the twentieth century, three quarters of Moscow's inhabitants had been born outside Moscow and two thirds were of peasant origin.

3   In 1912, the average number of residents per housing unit was 8.2 – compared to 3.9 in Berlin and 4.5 in London. This is further proof of the precarious conditions that Moscow's poorer classes lived under. R. Edelman, *Spartak Moscow: A History of the People's Team in the Worker's State* (New York: Cornell University Press, 2009), p. 27.

Together with his three brothers, he convinced his father to buy a football to be able to play in the courtyard of their apartment. The brothers went on to play with classmates and neighbourhood friends in vacant lots over the weekend. The presence of very many working-class youths in the same spot led the police to act out of fear that the gathering might become disorderly. They were banned from playing at weekends on the space by the cemetery where they used to meet. But that did not stop Chesnokov, who managed to find the money to rent some land near to Annengorfskoi Grove to be able to keep playing football. From among the regulars at these kickabouts emerged the founders of the *Rogozhsky Kruzhok Sporta* (Rogozhsky Sports Circle), the first workers' sports club (but which also included some students). Moreover, Chesnokov was responsible for organising the first 'wild football' competitions, which were met by hostility from the official Moscow League promotors. The contests ended in 1915, when the police stormed the Annengorfskoi field to break up the matches. Despite the attempts to negotiate continuing the matches with the security forces, eventually *Rogozhsky* ceased its sporting activity (due to the authorities rejecting any dialogue). Then, the indefatigable Chesnokov tried a merger with *Novogireyevo*, a club from the south east of Moscow. The latter rejected the offer, but it proposed that the best *Rogozhsky* players join its team. Their inclusion helped *Novogireyevo* put an end to the hegemony of *Morozovtsy*, which it beats, enabling it to win the local championship. It was the first time that a team entirely composed of homegrown Russians won the title – a success that had the knock-on effect of legitimising 'wild football'.

In Orekhovo – known as 'Russian football's third capital'– informal teams made up of workers also proliferated. There, each community had an improvised football team. Far from having the kits and footwear of the official teams, these 'wild footballers' would play with shoes, slippers, sandals, non-sporting boots, or even barefoot. For a ball they used rubber or leather skins stuffed with cloths or paper. Many players chose to skip breakfast and walk to where they had to go. That way, they would save a few kopeks, allowing them to buy reasonable-quality sports material. Such an attitude contrasted with that of the 'official' teams, such as *Morozovtsy*, who sucked up to their match referees by treating them at chic restaurants, such as Moscow's Metropole.

The banned worker teams would tend to adopt the name of the person in charge of organising them: for instance, the *Galkintsi* were promoted by Vladimir Galkin.[4] Another 'wild football' promoter, Gryzlov, had actively participated in the workers' movement as a member of the Russian Social-Democratic Workers' Party (RSDWP) – the organisation founded in Minsk in 1898. The teams backed by him and by Galkin, who was more inclined towards anarchism, took each other on for the first time on the Karasova pitch in 1909. The game ended in a 3–1 win for the team with RSDWP links.

Little by Little, 'wild football' spread among the employees of other factories belonging to Savva Morozov. That is how teams came to be set up such as the above-mentioned *Rogozhsky*,[5] Chibanov's Eagles – named after another worker

---

4   Pioneer in 'wild football' team creation. After studying at the Morozov factory school, he went to a higher-educational institution in St Petersburg. He later actively participated in the revolutionary movement in Orekhovo. Indeed, his parents' home was one of the Bolshevik safe houses in the area. In 1908, he organised a young workers' circle, some of whose members created the aforementioned football team.

5   To fund the team, the Vasilyev brothers sold buckets of water to their neighbours in the district, as it had no sewage or running-water systems. The team played on mud-laden fields and in cemeteries, and used logs as goalposts. Their most precious asset was the ball – the only one they had

in the RSWDP – and the squad Tanaev created with teenage employees in 1910. After exhausting ten-hour working days, people still found the strength to play football. Some of the teams would go as far as using empty potato sacks with holes to wear as football shirts. Other teams were known by their nicknames, such as the Bukanov Vikings, the Wild Ones, or the Tatars – named as such due to the west-central origin of the team's members (who also worked in a ceramics factory). There were even teams that took the name of the location of their playing field. These included Murzinka FC, a team made up of workers from Petrograd's Obukhov metallurgical plant – a factory created in 1863 to produce naval artillery using designs by the German firm Krupp.[6]

---

and which, each night, they carefully greased with fish oil. Their members' high playing ability attracted dozens of spectators, a development which worried the police. In those years, any workers' assemblies raised the suspicions of the authorities, the reason why police would tend to beat those coming to watch such matches. When, eventually, in 1914, the team was allowed in join official leagues, due to the team's impressive progress, it managed to beat *Morozovtsy* – the dominant team in the early years of Muscovite football.

6   The club was founded in 1914. Ten years later, coinciding with Petrograd's name being changed to Leningrad, it began being called *Volodarsky Raion* (Volodarsky District). The year after, it was renamed *Bolshevik* – the name by which the Obukhov factory itself was given then. From 1914 to 1924, *Murzinka* played its matches at the Obukhovsky Stadium. On the 23 September of the last of these years, it played its first match in the Leningrad championship. During the years of 1925 and 1926, talented players arrived at the club, such as goalkeeper Savintsev, defenders Shtukin and Kornilov, midfielder Popov, and the forwards Sykina, Yemelyanov, Rodionov, and Grigoriev. With them, *Bolshevik* became one of the city's strongest clubs. From 1927 to 1928, it was called *Klub Imeni V. I. Lenin*, but the subsequent next year it recovered the *Bolshevik* name (*Sportivny Klub Bolshevik*). In 1937, it won the Cup and the local League championship, enabling it to play in the USSR league. The following year, Mikhail Yudenich – a former Dynamo player – took charge of the club, which benefited from having players such as Golovnya (captain),

On many occasions, 'wild football' was the forerunner to the teams created in the factories. The former was the way by which workers got to know of the sport. Later, the playing was regulated by mainly British employees or managers. Football was brought by Britons, for instance, to Drezna, a town situated to the east of Moscow and named after the river there, where. Indeed, the place itself was created in 1897 to house the workers at a textile factory built by two sons of the industrialist Ivan Zimin – a native of Orekhovo-Zuevo. It was two company employees – its manager Eastwood and engineer Forns – that taught the workers how to play, in 1904. All the same, six more years were needed before the city's first football team was formed.

Another team made up of workers that took the name of their company was *Putilovsky*.[7] This came out of the Putilov munitions plant in Petrograd and its players trained at the Yekaterinhof Amateur Sports Circle facilities. When, in 1914, the authorities lifted the ban preventing the workers' teams from participating in formal competitions, both the above-mentioned *Murzinka* and *Putilovsky* registered to participate in the official leagues. They were not the only teams to take this step. In 1916, two more workers' clubs competed in the Petrograd championship: *Volga* – consisting of workers from the Alexandrov, Semyannikov, and Atlas factories – and *Pochtovo-telegrafniye chinovniki* (PTCh), the team for postal and telegraph employees. The decision to incorporate these teams was, at heart, due to the desire to improve Russian footballing standards.

Mikhailov, Zubarev, Ginko, Kicevo, Efimov, Trushkin, Tereshënok, Wallner, Nikiforov, Andreev, Sychev, and Krylov. It was one of the clubs that foreshadowed *Zenit*.

7   Remembered as the oldest workers' team in the country, after the 1917 Revolution it became called *Krasny Putilovets* (Red Putilovite), only later to be renamed *Kirovsky Zavod*, and, then, *Kirovets*.

9

The Impact of the 1914 Great War

In early 1912, General Voyeikov was appointed to direct sport and physical education in the country. On 15 March, in the first meeting he presided over for the Committee for the Physical Development of the Population of the Russian Empire (effectively a Ministry of Sport), it was decided to encourage the development of physical exercise and sport in Russia and exercise political control over it. The main aim was to mobilise and train citizens for the war seen as coming. The conflict, which Russia entered without being prepared for, with its discontented people and a discredited reigning family – inspired interest in people's physical instruction, given that 'tough and aggressive bodies were needed for the front'.[1] To bring that about, in 1915 the Committee issued an '[a]nnouncement on sporting mobilisation' and created special military committees that included representatives from the different existing sports organisations and clubs. The goal was to train 'the athlete to be a soldier, and vice-versa', and 'generate a civic attitude to produce fighting men that were physically and morally suitable'.[2] Additionally, different reports were produced by the

1 Riordan, *Sport in Soviet Society*, p. 112.
2 Nevertheless, these initiatives came too late. The response from the sports societies was not that which had been hoped for. Few clubs got involved, and some of the sports committees had already come under revolutionaries' control, such as the artillery-making workshops at the Putilov munitions plant. In 1917, the committee was taken over by the Bolsheviks, who turned it into a military training organisation operating under the name Vsevobuch.

Russian Olympic Committee and Lieutenant General Federov that highlighted the need to promote sport in order to improve people's physical condition. For that reason, the war effort became accompanied by the inclusion of physical-education courses in schools.

Until then, the Tsarist Empire had tried to limit and delay the spread of sport in the country. The link clubs had with the emerging proletariat produced misgivings among authorities that were wary about them becoming centres of revolutionary activity. For that reason, the state tried to dampen their growth. In the Empire's non-Russian territories, the fear was that the sports societies would become nationalist flagships, as had happened in Czechoslovakia with the Sokol gymnastics movement or in Germany, with its equivalent the *turnverein*. For that reason, when the start of the First World War (also known as the Great War) began to be seen as inevitable, the Empire's efforts at limiting sports clubs' expansion came too late. Indeed, already by 1914, there were 8000 registered football players across the Empire.

With both charitable and football-promotion ends, on 25 March that year a match between the two teams was held: one made up of *Morozovtsy* members – such as Charnock, Stepanov, and McDonald – and the other a mix of Muscovite-only players. Shortly after, on 7 April 1914, construction started on *Morozovtsy*'s stadium – one of the best grass-pitch grounds in the era and with a 10,000-spectator capacity. Brits were hired to oversee the technical aspects of the work. For its inauguration, a student team from the University of London was invited to play.[3] In the opening ceremony, holy water was sprinkled on the playing area, the stands, and stadium doors;

3   As well as the Moscow team's facilities being the best in Russia then, they were no second best to those of British clubs. *Morozovtsy* had an excellent pavilion with changing rooms, baths, a dining area, a large hall

5000 Muscovites would fill the terraces. The match ended with the visiting Britons winning 5–1. Match reports praised their game: 'They seemed to have the double the amount of players on the pitch. This lesson should not be missed by the *Morozovtsy* players'.[4] During their successful tour, the Londoners came away with wins from each of their matches.

By 1914, the Orekhovo league had 29 teams. These included the Pavlosky Sports Club, Glukhovsky Sports Circle, Abramova Factory Sports Circle, Dulevski Sports Circle, Podgnornaya, Labrina-Hraznova factory team, and Orekhovsky Sports Circle – the local traders' team. For its part, St Petersburg had 23 teams competing in its league, while in seven neighbouring districts as many as 34 clubs participated in what was known as the *Dacha* (Holiday Cottage) Cup.

Meanwhile, there were more and more requests to be able to participate in a national league. This interest came from cities and towns like Rostov, Chernihiv, Bogorodsk, Riga, Tver, Simferopol, Yelizavetgrad (now Kropyvnytskyi), and Yuzovka (today's Donetsk). But not all the news about Russian football was good. In June, the national team travelled to Malmo to compete in the Baltic Olympic Games. Differences between those governing football in Moscow and St Petersburg led in the end to no footballer from the capital going to Sweden. 'The saddest phenomenon in Russian sport. An act of personal vengeance at a time when everyone should be together in defending the national cause'; that was how the press described it at the time. In spite of winning the bronze medal, the Russians did not have a shining tournament, as demonstrated by their 7–0 defeat by Germany.

---

for social events, and even a cinema. Riordan, *Sport in Soviet Society*, pp. 34 and 35.

4 Text taken from https://bogorodsk-noginsk.ru/socium/21_futbol. html (last accessed: 18 February 2022).

Soon, rivals would become enemies. That summer, the First World War began. On 19 July, Tsar Nicholas II solemnly read the declaration of war at the Winter Palace. Straight away, demonstrations of patriotic fervour took place in the streets of Petrograd – the name that St Petersburg adopted on 31 August 1914 to avoid any Germanic reminiscences. Hostility towards the enemy was expressed in attacks against German shops and citizens. On the 20th, a multitude stormed the German embassy and killed one of its diplomatic corps.

In this context, hundreds of athletes and players went from training to picking up arms to defend the Empire's interests. This obviously affected sporting activities. Tournaments were cancelled and footballers called up. This way, *Morozovtsy* lost the Kynin brothers, Mishin, Savintsev, Volkov, and Maslov, who all went to 'defend Russia's honour'. Despite the outbreak of conflict and the suspension of championships in the towns nearest to the front, football matches continued to be played during the war. The last Cup fixture was played as late as August, with Russia already deep into its war campaign. The League continued until it was ended early in September. In Moscow, a city where the effects of the war were less punishing, the local champion was *Novogireyevo* – the first tournament winner that did not include any foreign players.

The conflict's effects, however, would lead to difficulties in finding pitches fit to play matches on. This circumstance was all the more difficult if the location was close to the front, as was the case with Petrograd. The shortage of playing fields had a lot to do with the hardships caused by the war, which meant, for example, that some pitches were turned into allotments to plant vegetables to feed the population, or were used to perform military drills. Despite all the obstacles, the match that traditionally pitted together the picks of both Petrograd and Moscow's best footballers kept being played during the Great War.

In 1915, there was an attempt to normalise footballing activity. Clubs prepared for a season that had to start in that spring. On 12 April, the first match was played. Profits from some matches were given to injured soldiers or donated to the Red Cross. The odd club, nonetheless, was forced out of the tournament after losing players for the war and being left short. Undoubtedly war propaganda had an effect on this: 'If you are healthy and can play football, you are strong and salubrious to fight on another field. Come and defend the fatherland'.[5]

That very year, as the conflict continued, the RFS renewed its governing board. At the meeting for this – held on 28 June – Georges A. Duperron was collectively chosen as president. Additionally, the meeting also made official the new Russian-language terminology applied to football, which would replace the very many Anglicisms still used then. Due to football's ascendancy, three divisions ended up existing. This meant that some matches would be played mid-week – on work days – which would limit participation by working-class players with families.

During the war, military sports committees were formed across the country. These were put in charge of training conscripts before they reached the front. During their training period, the emphasis was on physical education. On 3 April 2016, the first meeting of the Military Sports Committee of Russia was held. The aim was to link up with sports clubs and bodies and start a 'sporting mobilisation' campaign.

As well as the authorities' desire to control sport with a view to militarising it, the war caused other real problems for

---

5   Text taken from https://bogorodsk-noginsk.ru/socium/21_futbol. html (last accessed: 20 February 2022).

the football clubs. On top of having unstable line-ups due to players leaving for the front, the war hampered communication between cities, which would complicate teams' mobility. It, therefore, was common for squads to arrive late to matches thanks to problems during their trip.

In 1916, news came of the death of two more footballers on the battlefield: Second Lieutenant Shevelkin and Private Kurin. The military setbacks suffered by the Imperial Army also undermined morale in the rearguard, which harmed interest in football – as interest in it became eclipsed by the urgent problems the conflict produced. Footballers fell into passivity, with few clubs able to maintain their players' former attitude and drive. In order to overcome this mood and re-attract the public to the stadiums, benefit matches were held, in autumn 1916, and a regular sports paper only devoted to football, *Vestnik petrogradskoi futbol'noi ligi* (the Petrograd Football League Herald), began being published.[6] Meanwhile, given the context, the RFS reflected on the suitability of holding a national championship. The negative response to the idea from most clubs led the Federation to postpone holding such a league. Nonetheless, in Moscow the local club tournament was held, which was won by Zamoskvoretsky Sports Club (ZKS) – a team created on the banks of the Moskva river, to the south of the Kremlin.

The Great War left a river of blood on the Russian side.[7] As well as Shevelkin and Kurin, some of the footballers who had been in the Empire's team that competed at the Stockholm Games died as soldiers. One was Lieutenant Andrei Aleksandrovich Akimov. Born in Gorodishchi (Vladimir province),

6   Its first edition came out on 17 August 1916. Its publication continued until 1923, when its last edition saw the light of day.

7   During the Great War, of the nearly 15 million people called up to fight for the Imperial Army, two million perished.

this capped player was a very talented midfielder, the reason why he was considered to be a pillar of that generation of Russian football pioneers. From 1907 to 1908, he played for *Klub Sporta Orekhovo* (KSO), later to go on to wear the shirt of Orekhovo-Zuevo Sports Club until the military conflict began. Unfortunately, Akimov died in combat on the German front in 1916. This loss, though, was not a one-off incident. Another member of that Olympic delegation who died fighting on the front line was Nikolay Dmitriyevich Kynin. This forward, who was Akimov's teammate at KSO, also lost his life in 1916 on the Eastern Front. Kynin had been part of the team that in 1910 had won the first Moscow football championship – a success that would be repeated three times in a row. The last player in the aforementioned national squad to die in combat was Grigori ('*Gori*') Mikhailovich Nikitin. Born in St Petersburg, this capable goal-scorer, who played for Sport in his native city, lost his life in 1917 – the year of the October Revolution.

PART III

Youth

Юность

10

Tumultuous Times and the 1917 Revolution

The war sharpened the economic and political crisis suffered by the country, putting Russia in a critical situation between the years of 1916 and 1917. The military clash had scared off foreign investors and led most British employees to leave. Many returned to their country to voluntarily enlist in the British Army – a departure that left vacancies clubs would find difficult to fill. Yet this aided the rise of a new generation of less-experienced footballers.

Even in the middle of the conflict, the desire to keep playing football persisted. That explains why, despite the social and political dead-end the country was in, after the fall of the Tsar and the creation of the Provisional Government, several local tournaments continued to be played. These included the Fulda Cup in Moscow, won by *Novogireyevo*. Nor did victory by the Bolsheviks mean a total stoppage of footballing activity, particularly in cities such as Moscow. All the same, many players, referees, and promoters abandoned playing sport or stopped organising or refereeing matches.

But what was the Bolsheviks' real interest in sport in general and football in particular? Was it something relevant to them? Lenin, for instance, had played several sports in his youth: from hiking to cycling, ice skating, shooting, *gorodki* (a traditional skittles game played with a bat), and fishing – in which (according to his peers) he stood out for his impatience.

During his times in prison or exile, he valued sport as a mental stimulation to keep him taught and well-alert. When he was locked up in St Petersburg, he wrote that 'doing gymnastics gave me great pleasure and made me value the day'. In a letter sent from Munich to his sister he reminisced that doing such exercises 'is absolutely vital when you are alone'.[1] Lenin recognised sport's effects 'upon the social behaviour of citizens and upon the promotion of health'.[2] At the same time, he noted that sport could make a significant contribution to forming communist society's full individual and, through this, aid women's emancipation. With regards to this, the Bolshevik leader highlighted the importance of the task to be met by Vsevobuch: the compulsory training programme run by the General Administration of Universal Military Instruction – directed by the People's Commissariat of Military Affairs – which was introduced across the country in 1918. This was to establish a relationship of comradeship among young men and women. For him, sport was the ideal vehicle to attract women to public activity and through this more rapidly achieve equality.

1   Among his pastimes were skating, cycling, and skiing – a sport he did 'simply because he liked it'. His exile, trips and changes of city prevented the Bolshevik leader from living a healthy life or doing sport with some regularity. All the same, even though he never wrote any work related to sport, Lenin always believed that physical culture and the revolution were closely related. It was not for nothing that he became nicknamed the 'father of Soviet physical culture'. It was he who brought about the introduction of physical education in schools, which together with free hot meals and other measures, was to ensure a healthy lifestyle for Soviet children and teenagers. Lenin also was concerned about the health of workers and peasants because he said it was communists' duty to be so. M. Karpov, 'Упражнения с бревном' (Exercises with the Balance Beam), *Lenta.ru*, 15 June 2017.

2   J. Riordan, *Sport in Soviet Society. Development of Sport and Physical Education in Russia and the USSR* (London: Cambridge University Press, 1977), p. 63.

But Lenin's true passion was chess: a hobby shared with many other Russian émigré intellectuals and Karl Marx.[3] Indeed, he went as far as playing regular long-distance matches with playwright Anatoly Lunacharsky and writer Maxim Gorky, with whom he sent the movement of the pieces by post. Lenin's chess-playing was described by Alexander Bogdanoff, a Belorussian doctor and philosopher, as well as a theoretician of the *Proletkult* (Proletarian Culture) movement – created in February 1917 and aiming to radically modify art forms through creating a new proletarian culture linked to the Socialist Revolution. Bogdanoff sent a letter, penned on 19 November 1917, to Lunacharsky – his brother-in-law – saying that Lenin was 'a tough chess player'.[4]

The tasks corresponding to running a new state – as was 1917 Revolutionary Russia – forced Lenin to give up chess.

3   The German philosopher and theorist hated physical exercise and chess was the only sport he did during his life.

4   Born in Grodno, Belorussia, in 1873, Bogdanov studied medicine at Moscow State University. During his education, he was arrested for his connection with the *Narodnaya Volya* (People's Freedom). He graduated in 1899 and soon after was arrested by the Okhrana –Tsarist secret police – and imprisoned for six months. In 1903, he joined the Bolshevik faction of the Russian Social-Democratic Workers' Party (RSDWP). At one point, Bogdanov got to compete with Lenin over leadership of this wing. After the unsuccessful 1905 Revolution, both their stances began to diverge. In 1909, Lenin published *Materialism and Empirio-criticism*, a book in which he was very critical of his fellow comrade. Bogdanov was accused of following 'philosophical idealism'. In 1909, after the Bolshevik conference in Paris, he was expelled from the party. Then he joined his brother-in-law Lunacharsky and Maxim Gorky, who were on the Italian island of Capri. There, they promoted a college for workers until, in 1910, they moved to Bologna. Bogdanov would not return to Russia until 1914 and his abandonment of revolutionary activity – taking advantage of a political amnesty declared by Tsar Nicholas II coinciding with the Romanov Dynasty's Tercentenary. He would die on 7 April 1928, during an experiment, after performing a blood transfusion from a student of his who suffered from malaria and tuberculosis, to experiment with the potential immunological effects of such transfusions.

Matches tended to be long, and that meant too much of his time was taken up by it in his ever-packed schedule. The years in which he would stay captivated for a good while, thinking through his next move with his gaze fixed on the chessboard, had now gone. His duties – as head of the Council of People's Commissars for the RSFSR between 1917 and 1921 – would lead him to reluctantly and gradually detach himself from chess. All the same, in November 1922 he was named honorary president of Moscow's Chess Society in recognition of his fondness for the 'gymnastics of the mind'.

Despite not being able to enjoy sport like in previous years, Lenin did share related concerns with Nikolay Podvoisky – member of the Russian Social-Democratic Workers' Party, head of the Petrograd Revolutionary Military Committee in the October Revolution, and People's Commissar for Military Affairs until March 1918. Podvoisky, who also would be the first chairman of Vsevobuch and – between 1921 and 1923 – of the Sportintern (Red Sport International), acknowledged that Lenin had underlined the importance of training in fields such as horse-riding, skiing, cycling, and water sports, as well as the need to use that training in work and military environments. For Podvoisky, it was clear that 'it was impossible to bring the Civil War to a successful conclusion or to build socialism without a large-scale campaign to improve physical fitness and health'.[5] And all this had to be done urgently due to the fratricidal military conflict that broke out in late 1917.

Yet, in truth, beyond the interest of Lenin and some educators that, before the Revolution, had defended introducing a universal physical-education system, a good many Bolsheviks were little interested in the sport. The reason was the critical view they had of competitive sport, such as football,

5   Riordan, *Sport in Soviet Society*, p. 73.

which they took to be capitalist spectacles. Unsurprisingly they supported amateurism and opposed commercialism. All this was nothing new, if we bear in mind the attitude to sport shared by much of the left internationally at the time. An example can be found in the British Independent Labour Party, which had already warned in 1904 that 'we are in danger of producing a race of workers who only obey their masters and think about football'.[6] Far from being a one-off stance, this perception of football as an upper-class pastime that alienated the working class and 'turned it away from the class struggle' was pretty widespread on the European left in the early twentieth century. We find a similar instance in 1908, when we could read in the Newcastle paper *Northern Democrat*: 'The task of getting football out of people's heads and instilling socialism in them is difficult. But it is a task that must be attempted because if football is not important, socialism is very'. Yet, at heart, all of this is comprehensible if we take into account the problems that the revolutionary and socialist organisations had in not foreseeing the rise of sport. They were simply caught off-guard by its emergence and popularisation. Their paradox was that the areas with the best-organised working class in Britain (northern England, south Wales, and the west of Scotland) were where football and rugby had the biggest following.

To avoid the spreading of a phenomenon they did not control, the workers' organisations publicised calls stating that sport side-tracked workers from political activism and distracted them from the class struggle. Football, they said, 'sent the proletariat to sleep' and 'depoliticised workers'.

---

6   T. Mason, *Association Football and English Society, 1863–1915* (Brighton: Harvester Press, 1980), p. 237.

Anarchists also conveyed similar criticisms towards football. In 1917, the Argentinean libertarian newspaper *La Protesta* published an article against 'pernicious idiotising through repeated kicking of a round object'. Football, for them, was a kind of 'deviation'. They went as far as comparing it with religion: 'Mass and ball, the worst drug for the people'. On the other hand, the members of the *Club Mártires de Chicago* (Martyrs of Chicago Club – the forerunner to *Argentinos Juniors*) conceived football as the perfect metaphor for a socialist game based on solidarity. Indeed, the club's name itself was a homage to the eight workers that suffered cruel reprisals – five being condemned to death and the rest were jailed – for the Haymarket Riot (1886), the origin of the International Workers' Day commemorated on 1 May.

In contrast to this rejection of capitalist sport, the Bolsheviks gave quite some importance to widely promoting physical exercise. Lenin himself, as we mentioned earlier, recognised the 'transformative potential of physical culture as a means of obtaining the harmonious all-round development of the individual'.[7] This thesis was reasserted at the Third Congress of the Russian Young Communist League – also known as Komsomol – held in October 1920. At this was passed the resolution 'On the Militia Army and the Physical Education of Young People', stating that '[t]he physical culture of the younger generation is an essential element in the overall system of the communist upbringing of young people, aimed at creating harmoniously developed human beings, creative citizens of communist society'.[8] The statement concluded that '[t]oday, physical culture also has direct practical aims: (1) preparing

7   J. Riordan, *Sport, Politics and Communism (International Studies in the History of Sport)* (Manchester University Press, 1991), p. 4.
8   M. O'Mahony, *Sport in the USSR. Physical Culture – Visual Culture* (London: Reaktion Books, 2006), p. 15.

young people for work; and (2) preparing people for military defence of their country'.[9] During the Congress, young people were urged to 'acquire the necessary moral qualities to build a new socialist society' by means of promoting hygiene, exercise and discipline.

Furthermore, the Bolsheviks rejected being part of the Olympic movement as they saw it to be an elitist and bourgeois version of amateurism.[10] They, therefore, boycotted the Olympic Games, organising their own pro-worker sporting contests, such as the *Spartakiads*.[11] The Sportintern[12] planned the first *Spartakiad* to be held in Moscow in 1928 to herald both the beginning of the First Five-Year Plan and the tenth anniversary of the Soviet sports movement. Essentially the event aimed to fight for the hegemony of the international

---

9   Ibid.

10   The Soviet Union did not join the IOC until 1952, when, despite Cold War tensions, the USSR sent a delegation to participate in the Oslo Olympics. The Soviet Union's Olympic Committee was accepted into the IOC in the 45th session international body, held on 7 May 1951. Consequently, the USSR was able to sign up the sportspeople that were to represent the country in the XV Olympic Games.

11   It takes its name from Spartacus, the Thracian gladiator who led a slave uprising against the Roman Republic in 73 BC.

12   This body was created, in August 1921, during the Third Congress of the Communist International – otherwise known as the Third International or Comintern – held in Moscow. As well as discussing the creation of united fronts and the incorporation of women workers in the Communist movement, representatives of Soviet Russia, Germany, Czechoslovakia, France, Sweden, Italy, and Alsace-Lorraine participated in the founding of the International Association of Red Sports and Gymnastics Associations – commonly known as Red Sport International (RSI) or Sportintern. The idea had been discussed the year before, during the Second Congress of the Comintern, at the proposal of Nikolay Podvoisky, who became its first chairperson and who believed that physical training would benefit the Red Army. The new organisation proclaimed that 'sport was a political battlefield and the goal of the workers' movement was to contribute to the struggle for a[n international] revolution along similar lines to the October Revolution in Russia'.

workers' sports movement. This was in opposition to the International Association for Sports and Physical Culture – otherwise known as the Lucerne Sport International [translator's note: and later becoming the Socialist Workers' Sport International],[13] which had been organising the Workers' Olympiads since 1921.[14] On 12 August 1928, around 30,000 sportspeople paraded across Red Square, carrying red banners and flags while different bands played *The Internationale*.[15] The destination for the retinue was the Dynamo Stadium, where much of the *Spartakiad* would be held.

Far from fully rejecting sport, including football, the Bolsheviks reproached only its capitalist facet, which, for example, they identified in Coubertin's Olympics. Instead, they praised the benefits they understood were inherent to sport. As well as bettering people's health and physical condition, and the application of this in the military field, a section of the revolutionaries also extolled other values they associated with sport. Lenin himself, referring to the 'Christmas Truce' that took place in December 1914, during the Great War,

13   The name came from the Swiss city that hosted the organisation's founding meeting in September 1920. During this, the Belgian and French delegations asked for the name 'socialist' to be omitted from the organisation's name for it to attract a broader following.
14   Eventually, in August 1927, the two worker sports organisations definitively broke with each other, when the leaders of the social-democratic Second International banned their sportspersons from participating in the RSI-organised *Spartakiad* in Moscow. In Germany, thousands of sportspeople were expelled from the German branch of the Socialist Workers' Sport International.
15   Some sources reduce the figure for athletes participating in the inaugural ceremony to 4000. Among the participants were around 600 foreign students from a dozen countries that competed in the 21 fields – including football – programmed for these first Games. Alternately at the Olympic Games taking place in Amsterdam that year, the number fell to 17. At the end of that very year, the Winter Spartiakad was organised, with 628 participants competing at skiing, speed-skating or a biathlon.

defined that unofficial match played by British and German soldiers in the no-man's land between each side's trenches as an 'object lesson in internationalist fraternisation'.[16] On the other hand, Trotsky, who paradoxically would later be one of the main proponents of extending sports activity – due to the war requirements of the new socialist state – criticised the role of sport in his 1925 article 'Where is Britain Going?' He argued in this, 'social conventions, the church and the press, and ... sport had restricted and suppressed the possibilities for cultural enrichment available to the working class under capitalism'.[17]

Sport's biggest critics particularly emphasised their disapproval of professionalism and competitive sport, perceiving these as alien to socialist society and furthermore as distorting the 'eternal ideals' of physical education. They contended that competitive sport diverted the masses' attention from their main goal. Moreover, instead of sport providing people with healthy pleasure, it turned them into passive spectators.

After the October Revolution, the country's new authorities inherited from Tsarist Russia a young sporting movement which, despite having few facilities and little organisation, did have a centralised structure. This, as mentioned, was directed by General Voyeikov at the Office for Physical Development in the Russian Empire – the body responsible for militarising sport in the Empire's territories. With the Bolshevik's rise to power, this old body was replaced by a new one: the Central Board of Universal Military Training – better known as Vsevobuch due to its Russian initials. This took immediate control of the clubs in all sporting fields. The proposal to create this body had arisen during the Russian Communist

---

16 T. Collins, *Sport in Capitalist Society. A Short History* (Oxford: Routledge, 2013), p. 96.
17 Ibid.

Party's Seventh (Extraordinary) Congress held in Moscow from 6 to 8 March 1918. A subsequent decree passed by the Executive Central Committee named 'On Compulsory Education in the Art of War' rallied all workers aged between 16 and 40 to undergo military instruction at work. For women and teenagers (aged 16–17 years), course attendance was voluntary. Those made responsible for training citizens were the roughly 50,000 officers at the Central Division of Universal Military Training (TSOVVO), which depended on the Central Department of General Military Education. Nearly half of these instructors (17,428) were formerly Tsarist Army officers – making the authorities worry that they would take advantage of their position to spread counter-revolutionary propaganda. The issue became a priority for Podvoisky. After carrying out a purge of 'hostile' trainers and 'alien elements', the head of Vsevobuch tried to extend training (based on physical education and shooting practice) to all worker and peasant youth. That would have the incidental effect of involving local Soviets, unions, and the Komsomol in workers' military instruction.

The basic programme introduced consisted of two hours of daily training over eight weeks. Sessions included the fundamentals for handling light weapons, shooting, military logistics, trench digging, and use of hand grenades. The instruction became intensified from June, when conscription to the Red Army was broadened.[18] By the end of 1918, around

18   By 1919, Vsevobuch had overseen the militarily training of around 100,000 communist party and Komsomol members, 82,000 workers and over 730,000 peasants. During the Russian Civil War, the total figure for trainees rose to five million. In 1923, the instruction process was suspended. However, years later, an order to re-establish 'the universal military training of the USSR's citizens' was given. This was due to the outbreak of what became known as 'The Great Patriotic War' (1941–1945), which began on 17 September 1941 – little more than two months after

350 workplace-related sports groups had been set up, which involved two million people.[19] On 25 May the following year, the first companies taught at Vsevobuch paraded through Red Square under Lenin and Trotsky's watchful eyes.[20]

The system of compulsory military training introduced after the triumph of the Revolution, in a period full of improvisations and experiments, significatively contributed to the Red Army's consolidation and strengthening. And it did this while, at the same, decisively boosting the development of physical and sporting culture in the country. Its introduction was accompanied by several purges. Vsevobuch, in conjunction with the Komsomol, carried out relentless persecution of what were seen to be 'bourgeois sports organisations ... and ... the sports and gymnastics clubs of all class enemies'.[21] As well as

the beginning of the German invasion (Operation Barbarossa). The directive to implement this was issued by the Commission for the Defence of the State on 1 October that same year. On that occasion, as well, a Russian-language course to facilitate integration into the different units for conscripts from the Tajikistan and Azerbaijan Republics, who either did not know or had very basic notions of the language. See P. A. Golub, *Revolutsiya zashchischchaetsia. Opyt zashchity revolutsionnykh zavoevaniy Velikogo Oktiabria, 1917–1920* (Revolution is Being Defended. The Experience of Defending the Revolutionary Conquests of the Great October; Moscow: Politizdat, 1982), pp. 221–223.

19   In January 1921, the number of physical-culture groups had grown to 1419 – having 143,563 members in them in all; of these, 5500 (around 4 per cent) were women. In all, in the 1917–1920 period, nearly four and a half million Soviet citizens trained at Vsevobuch centres. This led to a demand for sports facilities that was covered by the building of nearly 2000 sports centres in 1921 thanks to the voluntary efforts of Komsomol members.

20   Two years after being introduced, the programme was broadened; increasing from an initial 96 hours to 576 hours in urban areas and 436 in rural ones. This increase was helped by the inclusion of new sports disciplines such as swimming, skiing, and football and other team sports. Another addition to the training was the reading of manuals on hygiene, anatomy and psychology.

21   Riordan, *Sport in Soviet Society*, p. 71.

involving physical instruction, the programme encouraged the identification of those attending with a local club to strengthen the collective spirit that the new socialist state wished to instil among its citizens. For that reason, football and other team sports were specifically promoted. Football, for instance, was introduced in military preparation centres and all clubs were recommended to include playing it. For the same reason, the local championships held before the Revolution continued to be played between 1918 and 1920, despite the precarious conditions stemming from the social and political context.

Consequently, in the beginning of the 1920s, the Soviet football scene went through an important metamorphosis. Counter-revolutionary clubs were closed and other societies were forced to change their name to adapt to the new times. Meanwhile, other clubs were forced to move neighbourhood or town. And new military sports clubs were set up in different factories, railway warehouses, and mines. These included *Klub Oktyabrskoy Revolutsy,* Kiev's *Raikomvod*, Moscow's *Goznak*, the *Burevestnik* (linked to university lecturers and students), *Daugava Riga* (the Latvian industry society), *Krasnoye Znamya* (Red Banner – related to textile workers), *Trudovye Rezervy* (Professional Technical School), *Urozhai* (Harvest), *Opytno-Pokazatel'naya Ploshchadka Vsevobucha* (OPPV, Vsevobuch Experimental Demonstration Site – founded in 1923 in Moscow), *Avangard* (heavy industry workers' society – forerunner to *Metalist Kharkiv,* and *Žalgiris* (Lithuanian industrial workers' team).

In order to distinguish between the sporting activity administered by the new authorities from the one existing in the pre-revolutionary period, the term *fizkultura* (Fk) was used. This originated from the expression *fizicheskaya kultura* (physical culture), which directly addressed issues of communist education and preparing the masses for labour and defence. That explains why it was promoted and incorporated into educational programmes aimed at students and workers. *Fizkultura* did not only consist of physical and gymnastic exercises but also spreading hygiene practices such as bathing. In the words of Nikolay Semashko, People's Commissar for Public Health, 'it was sport and educational and recreational physical activity that was not influenced by capitalism'.[22]

Among the first measures to be adopted, often in the midst of the prevailing chaos and uncertainty of the period, we find the following: the dismissal of the Boy Scouts,[23] the assimilation of the *Sokols* and *Maccabee* organisations, as well as the disbanding of the very many bourgeois sports clubs given their presumed counter-revolutionary potential.[24] Some of these decisions were later overturned, while others were not enforced.

The effects that the radical changes of late 1917 – the October Revolution and the subsequent start of the Civil War – had on the everyday and competitive life of the country's

22   J. C. Fernández Truán, 'El movimiento gimnástico del Este (2.ª parte)', *Apunts. Educación Física y Deportes*, 3rd quarter 2008, p. 13.

23   Children of between 10 and 15 years old were incorporated into the first groups of the Soviet Union's Young Pioneers Movement – the organisation created in 1922 and for which many instructors came from the dissolved scouting movement. The People's Commissar for Education Nadezhda Krupskaya – also Lenin's wife – dealt with this matter in her treatise 'Russian Union of the Communist Youth and Boy-Scoutism' – published in 1922.

24   This was hardly surprising when taking into account that during the Russian Civil War, members of the *Sokol* and scout groups had actively collaborated with the White Guard – the counter-revolutionary nationalist army that fought the Soviet forces. It was not for nothing that the Second Congress of the Komsomol in 1919 passed a special resolution urging the government to dissolve the Scouts Movement, considering it to be 'a purely bourgeois system of spiritual and physical indoctrination of young people in an imperialistic spirit'. Riordan, *Sport in Soviet Society*, pp. 71 and 72.

sporting organisations did not stop football championships from being played in the main cities. These continued between 1918 and 1920. All the same, the Revolution's consequences were soon visible. Clubs were intervened in and their facilities confiscated, such as those of *Morozovtsy*, whose headquarters, in November 1917, were turned into a people's reading room for those working in the local textile industry. Other clubs and associations were less fortunate and were disbanded.

The Moscow League had to reorganise itself, given that only 19 teams survived: a figure that gradually rose until the Russian Civil War prevented growth. On top of clubs disappearing, in this period a string of players transferred to other teams to play for more stable clubs and in good-condition facilities.

With hindsight, it is not therefore difficult to understand why Bolshevik-supporting footballers were a minority in the revolutionary period. And there were even fewer players that were Party cadre. Russia's leaving the Great War, in order for the revolutionaries to fulfil their previous promises of peace, sparked a new military confrontation involving several world powers. Football, therefore, was pushed back in importance.

Yet the effects of the Revolution were not only limited to the native population. As we described before, the Bolsheviks' victory led many Britons to decide to leave Russia and return to their home country. Unsurprisingly the Russian industries they owned or worked in were nationalised, while the new authorities made very clear that 'foreign workers were no longer welcome'.[25] In the end, the Charnock family members felt that they had to leave Russia.[26] One of them, Clement, was

25   Ibid., p. 67.
26   All the same, in the case of Henry Charnock, departure was not immediate. He stayed for some time after having sent his wife – a Latvian aristocrat – and family back to Britain. He left the country in 1919 when, warned by Menshevik and Bolshevik friends of the danger he was in (as

in fact arrested by the Cheka in 1918 and, later, deported to Britain.[27] Another, Billy – one of Orekhovo's most outstanding players and who in 1913 got to wear the captain's armband for the Russian Imperial team – fled to Mexico, later going to live in Spain. The only Charnock brother that stayed in Russia was Ted, who remained in the country until 1927, working as a commercial attaché for the British embassy in Moscow.[28]

The flight of foreign settlers directly affected the management of clubs and footballing bodies. Those who, until then, had been excluded from the sport's power structures – for being Russian – now took the reins. In this regard, we can state that the revolutionary triumph accelerated the 'nationalisation' of Russian football.

The fratricidal war between Reds and Whites did not end until 1923. During that time, an outline could be seen of the deep and radical restructuring of sport that would take place soon after it. Once the period of uncertainty was overcome, it was not long before the Revolution's impact on football clubs became visible. All of them suffered from the changed landscape. The new authorities decreed the disbanding of some teams, while the rest were forced to change their names

he would be arrested and probably shot), he chose to leave the country. His escape route was a train to Finland, from where he managed to get back to England. Paradoxically, in the twenties, the Soviet government invited him to return to Russia to manage state-owned cotton-goods factories. Charnock declined the offer. Instead of returning, he created several import and export agencies that traded with Eastern European countries. K. Baker, *Fathers of Football: Great Britons Who Took the Game to the World* (Durrington: Pitch Publishing, 2015) p. 67.

27   Once in his country, Clement Charnock continued to work in the textile sector. His company HQ was located in Altrincham – a town to the south west of Manchester. He published the book *The Roving Frame* and obtained four carding machine patents from 1931 to 1935.

28   Ted Charnock was alleged to have been an informant for the British Secret Intelligence Service (MI6) – an accusation he always denied.

and be attached to some state-related social stratum, factory, or union.[29] Most, however, were able to keep the colours of their respective kits and shields.

In such a way, the Muscovite KSO became dependent on the Interior Ministry and its head Felix Dzerzhinsky, a Polish Communist who had founded, in 1917, the Bolshevik secret police, the Cheka (the All-Russian Extraordinary Commission for Combating Counter-Revolution and Sabotage). Under police tutelage, the previous king of Russian football was renamed FC Moscow Dynamo[30] – in 1923 (the year the Russian Civil War ended). From then on, the police link led rival fans to label the Interior Ministry team '*musor*' (literally 'rubbish' but used in Russian criminal slang to refer to the police). All the same, some footballing institutions, such as the Russian Football Union or the Moscow Collegium of Referees, where able to keep their original name.

The 1917 events, however, froze the process by which football was limited to local elites, allowing playing it to extend to everybody. Police control of clandestine teams and resistance from the well-to-do against sharing 'its pastime' with working people came to an abrupt halt. Politically and socially, the consequences of the October Revolution were the implementation of the Bolshevik promises (of peace, land, and bread) – visible in both the agrarian reform and the signing of the Brest–Litovsk Treaty (which meant Russia pulling out of the Great War, among other things). Beyond that, they

29   Other clubs and sports movements survived for a while after 1917, such as *Sanitas*, the Moscow Bank Clerks' Sports Society, Moscow's Amateur Skiing Society, the Moscow Skiing Club, the *Maccabee* movement (of which the first local branch had been created in Odessa, in 1913) and the Scouts. Yet, later, in the 1920s, the effects of the Civil War led to their disappearance.

30   A name that, according to writer Maxim Gorky, expressed 'energy, motion, and power'.

also brought a kind of democratisation and Russification of football playing. Left behind were the bans, restrictions, and repression that tried to stop the sport from being popularised, homegrown players to be included in teams, and football's conversion into a true mass phenomenon. As historian Louise Reynolds wrote, '[b]y 1917 it was clear that sports was [sic] changing the nation, while simultaneously the nation was changing sports'.[31]

---

31   L. McReynolds, *Russia at Play. Leisure Activities at the End of the Tsarist Era* (New York: Cornell University, 2001), p. 112.

11

'White' Football – Conspiracy and Espionage

The uncertain context was fertile ground for scheming and spying. Aside from the intrigues involving the different revolutionary groups, the foreign powers also wanted first-hand knowledge of developments. One of the governments most keen to have the latest information to hand was the British. With this aim, it mobilised its diplomatic corps and formed a spy network on the ground, directed by the Secret Intelligence Service (SIS) – otherwise known as MI6: the military intelligence bureau operating outside the United Kingdom.

Despite being unsuccessful at establishing an operational system like Germany – one of the countries involved in the Great War – Britain did manage to introduce several agents into Russia. Through them, MI6 provided financial aid to prop up the Provisional Government, led – from July 1917 – by Alexander Kerensky. The undercover agents that were forced to constantly change identity, managed to permeate Red Army and secret police commissariats. They got as far as preparing a plan – albeit a failed one – to remove Lenin from power.

The British spy network, which extended from Moscow to the Asian city of Tashkent (today, capital of Uzbekistan), had a unique member: Pyotr Petrovich Sokolov. Born in 1890, this blond, stocky but athletic young man was one of the players for Unitas St Petersburg, for which he played in several national championships. The player, who normally played as a defender, was one of the members of that Russian Empire Olympic team that competed at the 1912 Stockholm Games; and Sokolov was capped five times for his country. He combined doing sport – boxing also – with studying law at St Petersburg University. At the age of 28, he was conscripted due to the outbreak of the First World War. In 1917, he graduated from the Peterhof school for infantry sub-officers, and would, later become a second lieutenant. In August of the following year, Sokolov – a dedicated monarchist who had seen his own family fall victim to the repression applied by the Bolsheviks on taking power – joined the White Guard – the armed wing of Russian counter-revolutionary forces.

It was then that he came into contact with MI6 and was recruited to work for it by agent Paul Dukes – known by his nickname 'The Man of a Hundred Faces' and who worked as a concert pianist and deputy conductor at the Petrograd Conservatoire. During the Civil War, Sokolov collaborated with the network enabling White Russians to escape to Finland. In 1922, he set up in Terijoki – a Finnish town on the Karelian isthmus (which in 1940 would pass into Soviet hands and be renamed Zelenogorsk). There, he trained a football team made up of Russian émigrés. Sokolov combined this activity with being an active member of the Russian All-Military Union (ROWS) – founded in 1924 by the White Army's commanding general Pyotr Wrangel.

In the late 1920s, seeing his safety threatened, Sokolov fled to Norway after rejecting offers to cooperate made by the State Political Directorate (OGPU) – the RSFSR's secret police. In 1936, he acquired Finnish nationality. Later, he fought in the Winter War (1939–1940) – when Finland was invaded by the USSR and lost ten per cent of its territory to it. In that conflict, Sokolov, who had captain's rank in the Finnish Army and used false names such as Kolberg, Simolin, Erikson, and Sokolowski, worked in the Propaganda Department for the General Staff of the Army, under the command of Kaarle 'Kalle' Aukusti Lehmus.

From 1941, Sokolov collaborated with the Germans as an intelligence trainer. He joined the Russian Liberation Army (ROA), a unit of anti-Communist volunteers led by general Andrey Vlasov – Red Army deserter and Russian Civil War veteran – and which would fight on the Oder Front. He took responsibility for visiting prison camps to recruit new ROA members and future agents to infiltrate the USSR.

In September 1944, aware that the Soviet counter-intelligence service intended to wipe him out, he fled to Sweden. There he changed identity – taking the name Peter Sahlin – and took up residence in Enköping, where he died in 1971 of a brain tumour. During his time in the country, he remained linked to football, being a masseur for Enköpings SK.

Sokolov, however, was not the only footballer who combined doing sport with spying and engaging in conspiracies. The British cabinet's desire to not miss anything regarding the evolution of the Revolution meant, as already mentioned, infiltrating Russia with a network of secret agents. Another such agent was the diplomat Robert Hill Bruce Lockhart.

Born in Scotland in 1887, Lockhart was recruited by the Foreign Office when he was 20 years old. In 1912, he was sent to Moscow to take up the post of Vice-Consul for the British delegation in the city. Yet, in fact, he was accommodating diplomatic work with modernising Britain's intelligence apparatus in the country.

The local press published several articles on Lockhart, who they mistakenly described as a great sportsman. Actually, the true sports lover was his brother John, a Cambridge cricket player and Scotland rugby international. The claim about Robert, all the same, aroused the interest of the Charnock brothers' Orekhovo-Zuevo. They were ever-willing to offer a place in the team to a football-loving fellow countryman as, in those years, signing a Brit was equated with footballing success. Far from rejecting the invitation, Lockhart, who was in no way hopeless with the ball, which is unsurprising, as his father had been a footballer, became the sixth Briton to join the Muscovite first team. The diplomat, however, confessed that this was not quite for him. This playing in a half-British and half-Russian team didn't quite convince him. And even less so as the Russians were workers at the Morozov-owned firm.

Despite everything, Lockhart overcame his reservations and played. The compatriots he played with included – as well as the Charnock brothers – McDonald, Greenwood, and the aforementioned Archibald Wavell. The latter would become the last Viceroy of India and, in the Second World War, command the British forces in the Middle East, but in 1911 was a military observer to the Russian Army. With such a squad, KSO soundly won the championship. The medal they – and their other teammates – were awarded for this is today on show at the National Library of Scotland.

In his memoirs, Lockhart shares an anecdote from when his KSO took on a German team in Moscow. One of the Germans, whom the diplomat remembered as being 'considerably bigger than our men' and who 'used their weight with unnecessary vigour', knocked over an English player aged just 17 and who was a nephew of the Charnock brothers. It was the fifth or sixth time that the German had done a wild tackle against this particular opponent and Lockhart was furious: 'I lost my temper and addressed him in language which I admit I should never have used in England'.[1] It was then that the referee – also German (as a courtesy to the visitors by the Russian Football Union) – threw at him in excellent English: 'Be careful. I heard what you said. If you use language like that again, I'll send you off'.[2] Quickly Lockhart, who had called on God to end the German's life, apologised. For the British vice-consul in Moscow to be sent off in a match for bad language was pretty unacceptable for a man of his position. Yet, in spite of that incident, Lockhart considered, 'my football experience with the Russian proletariat as a most valuable part of my Russian education'.[3]

Soon after, he was assigned to the Petrograd embassy, from where he informed the Foreign Office about the outbreak of the October Revolution. From among his reports, one stood out, which stated emphatically, 'if more sport had been played in Russia, the Winter Palace would never have been stormed'.[4] In January 1918, Lockhart went back to Moscow as the British diplomatic corps' top representative to continue reporting the news – including the outbreak of the Civil War to the Ministry of Foreign Affairs.

His name became associated with an unsuccessful plot to assassinate Lenin, on 31 August 1918, which involved Fanny Kaplan, a Jewish-origin Ukrainian revolutionary in the Socialist Revolutionary Party (SRS or SRs). The next day, the *Pravda* newspaper denounced the existence of an Anglo-French plot to eliminate the Bolshevik leader. In the pages the name Lockhart appeared. The former KSO player was therefore arrested and

---

1   R. H. B. Lockhart, *Memoirs of a British Agent* (Barnsley: Frontline Books, 2011), p. 68.

2   Ibid.

3   Ibid., p. 67.

4   T. Collins, *Sport in Capitalist Society. A Short History* (Oxford: Routledge, 2013), p. 96.

taken to the Lubyanka building – the headquarters of the Cheka (secret police). After being personally interrogated by Felix Dzerzhinsky, he was condemned to death. Yet the Briton escaped execution thanks to a prisoner exchange offered by his government to Russia's new authorities on 2 October. The person swapped for Lockhart was Maxim Litvinov, the supreme representative – handpicked by Lenin – of the new Bolshevik government in Britain. Despite not having been an official posting, because the British did not recognise the new Russian authorities, Litvinov had been arrested with the sole purpose of putting an end to Lockhart's captivity. In fact, the revolutionaries' triumph led to the British diplomatic corps' departure from the country.

In actual fact, Lockhart was part of a ring created by Sidney Reilly, a British secret agent known as 'the Ace of Spies' to make an attempt on Lenin's life and destabilise and overthrow the Bolshevik government. The two had met with prominent anti-Bolsheviks, such as Boris Savinkov, head of the Union for the Defence of the Motherland and Freedom (UDMF). Their plotting was also known to the US and French consulates' intelligence agents. While the coup was being prepared, the country's new authorities raided the British embassy, leading Reilly to flee. While the counter-revolutionary forces were being reorganised, Kaplan tried to kill Lenin. It was then that Cheka agents rushed the British embassy and arrested Lockhart.

As we have been said, in the end, Lockhart was traded for Litvinov. Once freed, he was warned that if he set foot in Russia again, he would be executed on the spot. Once abroad, Lockhart helped Trotsky after he began to be persecuted. During the Second World War, Lockhart did propaganda work and acted as a liaison between the British government and the exiled Czechoslovakian cabinet headed by Edvard Beneš.

12

Civil War and Sport's Militarisation

Since its creation, the Soviet Union was internationally isolated. Foreign powers tried to strangle it both politically and economically to hinder the institution of a revolutionary-socialist state. Thus, once the Great War ended, the victorious countries chose to intervene against revolutionary Russia. The Allies were opposed to Bolshevism for giving in to the Germans and, particularly, due to the danger of Europe becoming infected with socialism. That led to the involvement – albeit limited – of North American, French, Japanese, British, and Czechoslovakian troops in the Russian Civil War, as well as the imposition of an international blockade against the country.

In this context, the Bolsheviks commissioned Trotsky, then People's Commissar for War, to set up a Workers' and Peasants' Red Army (RKKA) able to take on the anti-revolutionary forces. Left behind were the Red Guard militias that had defended the Revolution, a voluntary force that had disobeyed the officer class to side with the uprising. Now, the need was to build as disciplined and diligent a regular army as possible.

On 28 January 1918, the Council of People's Commissars formalised – by decree – the creation of the Red Army. Three months later, compulsory military service was introduced. The new armed force, which completely identified with Bolshevik policies, included former Imperial Army officers. These brought with them their knowledge and experience of combat, as was the case with the Latvian ex-Colonel Jukums Vācietis, who became Soviet Russia's military commander-in-chief (*glavcom*). His inclusion, however, created misgivings, which led to the introduction of the figure of military commissioner (later called political commissar), who had to oversee the former officers' loyalty.

The training of peasants, the strong discipline imposed (as summarised in the slogan 'threats, organisation and reprisals', aimed at those who might try and desert), the military instruction given by former Tsarist officers, and the enormous resources the army was given were vital to enable the Bolsheviks to change the course of the war from 1920. (Although we must add to these factors, the withdrawal of foreign troops – due to the conflict's protraction – and the infighting between White Army leaders.)

Also relevant was the fact that the Bolsheviks chose to direct and spread physical activity among citizens through the above-mentioned *fizkultura*, thus providing soldiers that were better prepared for fighting. Encouraging sporting activity became one of the measures used to increase Red Army soldiers' combativeness. Therefore, many Bolsheviks went from underestimating sport to seeing it as a crucial tool for winning the war.

In May 1918, a system of physical-education courses and schools was introduced, seeking to improve the fitness of enlist-ees. The institution entrusted with guaranteeing the initiative's success was the *Vseobshchee Voennoe Obuchenie* (Central Agency for Universal Military Training) – the aforementioned Vsevobuch. It was given the task of urgently supplying the Red Army with draftee intakes that were physically and militarily prepared to defend the Socialist state. It was created two months earlier, at the Bolshevik Party's Seventh Congress. Although initially it was aimed at workers, by the summer of 1918 it was extended to include peasants.[1] Its main goal was to 'prepare [civilian youth] physically and mentally for military action'[2] – something that was understood to be 'essential to success on the battlefield'.[3] To achieve this, it set up Vsevobuch branches around the country, each of which created its own military committee. Furthermore, the new body controlled all of the existing sporting societies and clubs, and coordinated actions to physically train those that could be drafted.[4]

During the war, Vsevobuch did campaigns to promote the spread, alongside physical exercise, of good hygiene and nutritional habits. Its slogans were 'Help the Country with a Toothbrush', 'Help the Country by Washing in Cold Water', 'Help the Country by Observing the Dry [i.e. prohibition] Law', and 'Physical Culture 24 Hours a Day'.[5]

Nevertheless, their implementation was uneven, given the lack of sports instructors and equipment.[6] Priority was given

1   The programme was cancelled in 1923. The German offensive in 1941 led it to be relaunched thanks to a State Defence Committee passed on 17 September that year. It is calculated that during the years it was in effect – 1941–1945 – 9,862,000 men aged from 16 to 50 went through Vsevobuch. Standing out from among its instructors were those who would play an important role in the history of Spartak Moscow, such as the Artemyev footballer brothers, or the managers Konstantin Kvashnin and Mikhail Kozlov. Under the latter coach, the Muscovite team won its first Soviet Union championship: the 1936 autumn tournament when it beat Moscow Dynamo and Dinamo Tbilisi.

2   S. Grant, *Physical Culture and Sport in Soviet Society. Propaganda, Acculturation and Transformation in the 1920s and 1930s* (New York: Routledge, 2013), pp. 30 and 31.

3   R. Edelman, *Spartak Moscow: A History of the People's Team in the Workers' State* (New York: Cornell University Press, 2009), p. 43.

4   As well as doing sport, the Byelorussian branches programmed four military training sessions a week.

5   Riordan, *Sport in Soviet Society*, p. 73.

6   The shortage of facilities led it to order the local Vsevobuch branches to build the necessary venues for their activities to be carried out. This meant falling back on *subbotniki* (voluntary work carried out after work

to sports such as track and field, swimming, wrestling, fencing, and equestrian sports because of the clear military benefits that could be acquired from these. Football, on the other hand, was side-lined due to its 'unpredictability and occasional violence',[7] for which it was deemed inappropriate for the training and disciplining of soldiers. For that reason, soccer played a secondary role in the official Soviet sporting activity of the period. Despite these directives, however, football was a notable presence in the Vsevobuch centres thanks to draftees who, to get over training sessions seeking to instil discipline and respect for authority, played it in their spare time.

or during people's day off – originally Saturday (hence its name, which comes from the Russian word for Saturday: '*subbota*'). On top of that, sports material was officially confiscated from clubs or societies such as the *Sokol*, *Maccabee*, *Shevardeniya*, or Scouts.

7   Edelman, *Spartak Moscow*, p. 43.

13

The Third-International Team

Obviously, the events that shook the ancient Russian Empire aroused the international community's interest. Participation by 14 allied countries in the conflict in support of the Whites also grabbed the attention of the foreign press. Some newspapers sent correspondents to cover the Revolutionary victory and the ensuing civil conflict. One of the journalists on the ground was the North American John Reed. Known worldwide for his famous chronicle of the October Revolution, the book *Ten Days that Shook the World*,[1] Reed was also a sports fan. He did swimming and water polo and even had a trial for the Harvard football team.

In the middle of the war, the journalist played a leading role in a little-known episode, as he was in the starting eleven playing Russia's first 'international' football match since the Russian Revolution. Reed, who on that July day played as goalkeeper, did so in the same team as the Scottish trade unionist William Gallacher,[2] who was captain of a very *sui generis* team which

1   The volume has been edited in many languages. In 2017, coinciding with the centenary of the Russian Revolution, at least four different versions of the book in Catalan were published – thanks to the publisher Edicions de 1984.

2   Born in Paisley (Scotland) on 25 December 1881, son of an Irish father and Scottish mother, Gallacher began working at the age of ten and dropped out of school two years later. His father's alcoholism led him to become an activist in the Temperance Movement, which fought against drinking alcohol and promoted complete abstinence. By 1914, Gallacher worked at Glasgow's Albion Motor Works. He was briefly a member

was named International XI for the occasion. This was a squad made up of delegates and observers attending the Second World Congress of the Third International – the body created on Lenin's initiative, on 2 March 1919, and that brought together the different communist parties in existence. It played against a selection of Muscovite players, which hammered its opponents by a whopping 16–0. The event was the main item in a 'gymnastics' day held to coincide with the Comintern Congress, and which 18,000 attended. It took place in the area where Vsevobuch planned to build the new Red Stadium, in which previously the Moskva Swimming Club was based.

The initiative to play the match came from Nicolai Podvoisky, then the visible head of Soviet sport, who had written to Gallacher requesting that he choose eleven players from among the Congress delegates and their cohorts to make up a team. Among those chosen to represent the so-called International XI – the Third-International team – are key people such as the Englander Tom Quelch (member of the British Socialist Party, BSP); Jack Tanner (representative of the

of the Independent Labour Party until he joined the Social Democratic Federation. As a member of the Clyde Workers' Committee, Gallacher opposed Britain's entry into the World War. His involvement in the campaign to boycott the official Munitions of War Act (1915) led him to be given a six-month prison sentence. The notoriety that he gained for this led the Soviet authorities to invite him, alongside John Smith Clarke, to be a representative of the Scottish Workers' Committee at the Second World Congress of the Comintern. This event was held in Petrograd and Moscow in the summer of 1920 and attended by over 200 delegates from around the world. Lenin – who Gallacher even had a one-to-one meeting with – wanted to convince the two Brits of the need to create a united communist party in Britain. The CPGB would later be the result of this, with Gallacher being one of its main figures. In 1935, he was elected to the House of Commons. He died in his town of birth at the age of 83. See K. Morgan, G. Cohen, and A. Flinn (eds.) *Agent of Revolution: New Biographical Approaches to the History of International Communism in the Age of Lenin and Stalin* (Bern: Peter Lang Publishing, 2005), pp. 133–153.

Shop Stewards' Movement); Richard Clyde Beech (delegate of the British section of the IWW – the Industrial Workers of the World, the international union founded in the United States in 1905);[3] John ('Jack') Thomas Murphy (union organiser from Greater Manchester who also represented the Stop Stewards' Movement and who had entered the country illegally in January that year); as well as two German delegates; and five more who came from the United States. Among the latter, as well as the above-mentioned Reed (who, just three months later, would die in Moscow after catching typhus), there was Joe Chaplin, Joe Fineberg (veteran communist British Socialist Party representative and the person who really put the team together), Eadmon ('Eddie') McAlpine (delegate of the American Communist Labor Party, CLP), and David Ramsey. Once the match had ended, the winning Muscovite squad was awarded a prize by the organisers, which consisted of a jar of fruit and a bag of flour for each player.

As to the progress of the war, in 1921, the final offensive began – after the withdrawal of foreign troops the previous November – which ended successfully a year later. The Red Army became the weapon that in practice had saved the Revolution. Thanks to the conflict ending, football stopped being a fringe activity. The country was devastated by war.

---

3   We should mention, anecdotally, that Beech was married to the doctor Moira Elizabeth Connolly, daughter of James Connolly, the Irish nationalist leader. Her father had founded the Irish Socialist Republican Party in 1886 and was one of the few European left-wing leaders strongly opposed to the First World War. Lenin, who admired Connolly despite not having met him personally, defended the 1916 Easter Rising against those critical voices who argued that it was a bourgeois revolt. One of Connolly's five other children, Roderick (or 'Roddy') James Connolly, participated in the Second Congress of the Comintern as delegate for the Irish section of the IWW union. In October 1921, Roddy Connolly became the first president of the Communist Party of Ireland (CPI).

Tens of thousands of people had caught typhus. Tuberculosis and cholera also laid waste to a debilitated people. Drought, famine, and mass exoduses of people made the situation even worse. Consequently, the Bolsheviks decided to promote physical education with the aim of improving the welfare and health of Soviet citizens.

In this context of physical-education promotion, after adapting to and surviving the adversities of war, football became the most attractive sporting activity for working-class youth and adults. Although office and shop clerks were part of the mass of football lovers, its predominant consistency was proletarian. Those called the 'NEP football fans' – referring to the New Economic Policy put forward by Lenin to avoid the Soviet economy collapsing – were characterised by being 'dressed very simply and pretty much the same, wearing Russian-style shirts and jackets with their pants stuffed into the top of their boots'; 'the public was the simplest possible'.[4]

The victory in the Civil War increased the ascendancy and reputation of the Red Army in Soviet society. The conflict's end had the knock-on effect of Vsevobuch being shut down. From then on, the responsibility of watching over the development of the *fizkultura* programme was given to the workers' movement – including the unions. At the same time, the state military apparatus was allowed to continue directing its own clubs.

---

4   R. Edelman, *Spartak Moscow: A History of the People's Team in the Workers' State* (New York: Cornell University Press, 2009), p. 49.

14

Hygienists, *Proletkultists*, and the Concretisation of a Sports Model

In the middle of implementing the NEP, the country's sports structures were reorganised. It was a period marked by heated debates involving the Komsomol, unions, Hygienists, and supporters of *Proletkult*. It also was characterised by the attempts to create sports contacts internationally. The Hygienists were actually very critical of the militarisation of sport, which they saw to be excessive, and also of the emphasis on its competitive side, which they saw as harmful to health – both physical and mental.

The Supreme Council of Physical Culture (VSFK) succeeded Vsevobuch as the main governing body for Soviet sport. Created in the early 1920s by the General Military Instruction Service, which had directed physical education since the October Revolution, the VSFK was commissioned to lay down the foundations of the new Soviet sport. The football clubs, for instance, were organised according to what was named 'Promotion of territorial production', which aimed to push back the emerging professionalism that was identified with capitalism.[1] The new organisation made club players

---

1   In spite of impediments, from the 1920s on, the amateur Soviet foot-ball world did not stop having hidden professionalism. Under-the-table payments and awarding of privileges, such as having the best housing, was common practice by clubs in order to attract or retain players. Paradoxically, some footballers that were tied to clubs subject to their professional activity (soldiers in the Army team, Interior Ministry

have to be from the same district or factory in order to avoid transfers and signings. From April 1923, a month before the Twelfth Congress of the Russian Communist Party, it also was agreed that the disbanded teams be re-founded under new names. Behind this decision was the Party's will to progressively increase control over sport and reduce the autonomy of sporting organisations through ties to the unions and the Komsomol,[2] which acted as transmission belts to the working class and youth, respectively.[3]

Behind all this was the heated debate in the 1920s between the Hygienists – the followers of Lesgaft's theories – and supporters of the *Proletkult* thesis. While the former group had a view of sport closer to nineteenth-century reality, the latter wanted to promote a new proletarian physical culture.

One of the main bones of contention between the two tendencies was regarding competitions. The Hygienists

---

employees in Dynamo ...), changed jobs in the pre-season period – 'miraculously' so according to the media. Such unofficial transfers were the way used to go and play for another club. Despite all the evidence to the contrary, the authorities continued to deny the existence of professionalism in the USSR: 'The Soviet sportsman has no need to exchange seconds or centimetres of his records for coins; he has no need to 'make money' out of his football', in M. O'Mahony, *Sport in the USSR. Physical Culture – Visual Culture* (London: Reaktion Books, 2006), p. 68.

2   The measure also was aimed to reduce Komsomol's influence over sport. This was due to it having its own clubs, such as the *Muravei* Sports Societies, established in Moscow and Vladimir; the different *Spartaks* – not to be confused with the later Muscovite football club of the same name – in Petrograd, Novgorod, and Ukraine; or the *Krasny Molodniak* (Red Youth Societies) set up in Minsk and the Vitebsk province (Belorussia).

3   Indeed, it was on 13 July 1925 that the Party made public a resolution outlining the functions that sport and physical culture should have: ensuring politicisation, avoiding club autonomy, reaffirming Party leadership, and developing alliances between the workers' movement and the countryside, among other aspects.

admitted the usefulness of some 'bourgeois sports' – to use the vocabulary of the period.[4] On the other hand, the *Proletkultists* were stringent about not making concessions to such. For that movement, competitiveness (or 'champion mania') was an alien value to socialism. Therefore, as well as condemning certain sporting activities (boxing,[5] weightlifting, and gymnastics), which they saw as 'irrational and dangerous individual activities' more befitting of capitalism (because they prioritised rivalry over the values of health and physical culture), the *Proletkultists* proposed an alternative model. As well as mass performances that tried to exhibit the harmonic discipline of Soviet society – partly based on the *Sokol* gymnastics model – they also designed new games with ideologically suggestive titles, like 'Rescue from fascists', 'Agitators', and 'Helping the proletarians'.

Pressure from the Hygienists meant that in the first half of the 1920s, the country's authorities agreed to reduce the number of competitions and exclude some sporting fields from these. Thus, medical arguments and so-called 'labour gymnastics' won out, limiting the focus of sport to health and hygiene, while competitions and sport's educational and recreational aspects were side-lined. Resultingly, in the first Trade Union Games, held in 1925, some of the country's most popular sports, including football and boxing, were excluded from the official programme because they were considered 'of competitive nature'. In contrast, the most 'apt' or appropriate sports, in their opinion, were track and field, rowing and swimming (because these involved racing against the clock, rather than opponents).

---

4   Until 1945, Soviet sportspeople did not take part in 'bourgeois sports' competitions, apart from in fields such as chess or speed skating.

5   Around that time, boxing was banned in Leningrad city by order of the local government's Council of Physical Culture.

From then, however, increased Communist Party inter-ventionism in sport decreased the Hygienists' influence. The authorities, aware of their growing importance and of the state of confusion there was over the social function that sport should play in the USSR, decided to act. In a document made public in July 1925, the Hygienists were officially banished from Soviet sport's policy-making bodies.[6] Other factors would affect their increasing ostracism, including the ties they had with Lev Trotsky – then a declining figure in the Party. Accordingly, the most prominent Hygienists suffered similar persecution to that which the Trotskyists were subjected to. These were first expelled from the political organisation and, later, arrested, convicted, imprisoned, exiled, or executed.[7] Among those who suffered repression was doctor Zigmund, who opposed football because it was an unhealthy and little-educational sport. Zigmund was dismissed from his post at the Central State Institute of Physical Culture in Moscow for being believed to be a supporter of Trotsky.

6   The text explained that '[p]hysical culture must be considered not simply from the standpoint of public health and physical education, not only as an aspect of the cultural, economic and military training of young people … It should also be seen as a method of educating the masses (inasmuch as it develops will power and builds up team work, endurance, resourcefulness and other valuable qualities). It must be regarded, moreover, as a means of rallying the bulk of the workers and peasants to the various Party, Soviet and trade union organisations, through which they can be drawn into social and political activity … Physical culture must be an inseparable part of overall political and cultural upbringing and education, and of public health'. Reproduced in Riordan, *Sport in Soviet Society*, p. 106.

7   In 1936, the Central Committee of the Russian Communist Party declared that the approach advocated by many Hygienists was a pseudoscience and banned its practise. Their theories would not resurface until the 1970s, when German and French neo-Marxists called for the banning of sports – a thesis that Soviet theorists ridiculed as childish and deviationist.

As for the *Proletkultists*, they demanded rejection of competitive sport and all those sports activities they saw as having originated in bourgeois society, as these were perceived as '[r]emnants of the decadent past and emanations of degenerate bourgeois culture'.[8] The model they wished to impose aimed to be a revolutionary innovation in physical culture that sought the perfect proletarian body. It was based on what was called 'labour gymnastics': a series of physical exercises performed using different equipment with which young workers could emulate the physical tasks of their workplaces. These kinds of enactments, together with the creativity used when developing new games, led the *Proletkultists* to be accused of promoting a 'theatricalisation of sport'.[9]

Among the figures who dissented from the *Proletkult* ideas was Lenin himself. He did not see 'inventing' a new proletarian culture to be pertinent, but rather was inclined to develop as best as possible the 'forms, traditions and results of existing culture from the viewpoint of Marxist philosophy, and the living conditions and struggle of the proletariat'.[10] Other detractors maintained that there were not that many differences between the bourgeois clubs and proletarian sports, and that there was only a bourgeois attitude and proletarian attitude to sport.

Despite all the clear differences in approach, several *Proletkultist* proposals – such as to do what was called 'production gymnastics' – were incorporated into the Soviet sports model, even while some of its proponents were side-lined from public activity and the decision-making centres of the state apparatus. The First Five-Year Plan (1928–1932), introduced to favour the establishment of heavy industry in the country,

8   Riordan, *Sport in Soviet Society*, p. 101.

9   Ibid., p. 102.

10   Ibid., p. 103.

which also was aided by agrarian reform and land collectivisation, incorporated in it some of the ideas presented by the *Proletkultists* at some point. In the hands of the authorities, sport became a tool to fight disorderly and anti-Soviet conduct in the cities and the rest of the country. In rural areas, it was used to promote campaigns against drunkenness and anti-social behaviour among the youth. The Party saw it as an ideal instrument for putting its social policies into practice, contributing to the emancipation of the Soviet woman, and demonstrating the Soviet state's potential. From then on, the main goal was 'beating all bourgeois sports records'[11] in order to show, through sport, the supremacy of socialism over capitalism. In the process, it would make 'make [people] forget about domestic economic hardships' being suffered.

The criticisms of the sporting model introduced as a result of the triumph of the October Revolution went, however, beyond the hard debates between Hygienists and *Proletkultists*. Komsomol also was not in agreement with the way sport was evolving. In October 1920, it warned of the 'revival of the bourgeois sports clubs' and of the effects of sporting competitions, which, according to Komsomol members, 'breed, in some people's minds, attitudes alien to socialist society'.[12] With regards to football, the Communist youth organisation highlighted the harmful effects of rivalry. Its discourse equated football with the predominant economic system in Western countries, given that the 'players competing to score goals looked too much like capitalists competing to control markets'.

At its Fourth Congress, Komsomol began to openly attack Vsevobuch directives and the pseudo-professional elitism that

---

11   J. C. Fernández Truán, 'El movimiento gimnástico del Este (2.ª parte)', p. 17.
12   A. Guttmann, *Sport: The First Five Millennia* (Amherst: University of Massachusetts Press, 2007), p. 299.

had been instituted in sport. The fight to control sport was obvious enough in the upper echelons of the socialist state. Komsomol took the initiative to try to resolve this through understanding, which led the aforementioned Supreme Council of Physical Culture (VSFK) to be constituted. On 13 July 1925, the Council published its first resolution in which it outlined the tasks it had been assigned to perform (politicising sport, leading the setting up of sports associations, and creating a mass movement). The body, presided over until 1930 by Nikolay Semashko – a doctor by profession[13] – was made up of a representative from each of the People's Commissariats, a Komosol delegate, another from the All-Russia Central Council of Trade Unions, and a last member from the Moscow Soviet. The differences in opinion and quarrels over the control of sport continued, however. An overhaul of the whole organisational structure of Soviet sport was put forward during the Eighth Congress of the Komsomol, in 1928. This was because it was considered that the VSFK was incapable of enforcing an effective system of administration and control.

---

13   It was Semashko who promoted sporting activity as the means by which to eradicate so-called anti-social and anti-Soviet phenomena, such as prostitution, crime and alcoholism. He also used it to fight illiteracy among the population. Fernández Truán, 'El movimiento gimnástico del Este (2ª parte)', p. 18.

15

Isolation and Diplomacy, a Team at the Country's Service

The White's defeat in the Civil War and fear of world revolution led – as previously mentioned – the Western powers that had actively collaborated with the counter-revolutionary forces during the conflict to isolate the Socialist state born from the October Revolution. The fear that socialism's seed would germinate in their own countries inspired this blockade, something that Trotsky had predicted at the time: 'The Russian Revolution will create a storm in the West and all countries' capitalists will throttle our struggle'.[1] For practically two decades, the USSR ended up internationally isolated. This added to the destruction caused by the Civil War, which had devastated the country. In such a context, which forced the authorities to put the Soviet state's preservation before anything else, they used football as a launching pad to rebuild relations.

Participation in international-level sports competitions was sought to break the detachment of the Soviet Union – created in 1922 – while making clear the superiority of communism over capitalism – through the Soviet team and clubs' victories. From then on, wins would be interpreted and exploited in terms of politics. The government also hoped that competing abroad would help improve the standard of Soviet football.

1   M. Milosevich, *Breve historia de la Revolución Rusa* (Barcelona: Galaxia Gutenberg, 2017), p. 18.

There were two paths by which football could make contact with the outside world: international matches played by the different clubs or games involving the national squad (the *Sbornaya*). Rivals were local or national squads located close to the USSR's borders. Thus, the Soviet team played against Finland, Turkey, and Sweden, and teams such as Odessa, Leningrad, and Baku (Azerbaijan) competed, respectively, against the Iranian and Turkish squads, and a mix of players from Finnish clubs.

The first international fixture involving a team from the USSR was in 1922, when *Klub Sporta* played against the Finnish Workers' Sports Federation (TUL), who were on tour in Russia.[2] The game, which ended with a 7–1 home victory, was Soviet sport's first international event since the October Revolution.

Paradoxically – given the preceding history between Finland and Russia[3] – the following year, two Soviet teams played a

2   Organisation founded on 26 January 1919 by 56 clubs linked to the workers' movement – around both the Finnish Social Democratic Party and the Communist Party. This mix led to internal fights between Social-Democratic and Communist members. It was not until 1927 that the former group became hegemonic. Apart from competitive sports, the Federation promoted sports-related activities in education, aimed at young people. It was part of the Finnish Olympic Committee and the International Workers in Sports Confederation (CSIT). It reached having around 280,000 members and 1000 affiliated organisations in 59 sporting fields. In 1920, it became a founding member of the Socialist Workers' Sport International and, later, formed bonds with Red Sport International, enabling Finnish sportspeople to participate in both the Workers' Olympiads and the *Spartakiads*. The differences between the Social Democrats and Communists led the organisation to split, in December 1929, and for the second of the two parties to create a parallel body: the Unification Committee of Labour Sports.

3   The Grand Duchy of Finland had been part of the Russian Empire between 1809 and 1917. Yet it took advantage of the revolutionary outbreak to proclaim its independence at the end of the latter year. Then, Finland

full five matches in Finland – in the towns and cities of Kotka, Turku, Kuopio, Helsinki, and Tampere. Their superiority was crushing: they hammered the local teams with score-lines such as 19–0 and 13–1.[4] In symbolic terms, the poundings were a kind of payback by the Soviets who had been dogged by the humiliating defeat in the Stockholm games held a decade before. In spite of having gone to war with each other, and the Finns having refused to sign the nonaggression pact offered to them by the USSR, football became a peace-making tool. It helped restore relations between both countries, even if only in the sporting arena.

Despite its desire to play abroad, initially the Soviet football team only played against foreign 'workers' teams' due to FIFA rules preventing its members from playing against teams that were not associated with the international governing body. In August 1923[5] – only nine months after the Soviet Union was

---

participated in the Russian Civil War, working with the counter-revolutionary forces. General Carl Gustaf Emil Mannerheim, a former Russian Imperial Army official, was made chief commander of the Finnish forces that – with German support – fought against the Soviet troops.

4 The games between Soviet clubs and Finnish teams would last until 1929. The overall balance from the 16 matches played was clearly favourable to the Soviets: ten wins, three defeats, and three draws.

5 That same year, the Supreme Council of Physical Culture (VSFK) was created, the body responsible for reforming the country's sports structure. It was incorporated in the Ministry of Health, headed by Nikolay Semashko, People's Commissar for Public Health, a post he held from 1918 to 1930. In 1893, Semashko had begun his trajectory as active Marxist. In 1901, he graduated from the Faculty of Medicine at Kazan University. During the 1905 Revolution, four years later, he was one of the organisers of the strike at the Sormovo factory, for which he was arrested. He emigrated to Switzerland, where he met with Lenin. He was Bolshevik delegate at the International Socialist Congress held in Geneva in August 1907. After a time in France, Serbia and Bulgaria, he returned to Russia in 1917, becoming president of the Bolshevik faction in the Pyatnitskaya district. He participated in armed insurrection in Moscow and organised back-up medical assistance for the wounded. As a result

constituted – the Russian Soviet Federated Socialist Republic (RSFSR) was invited to play ten friendly matches by members of the old Swedish Workers Union (SVA) and the newspaper *Folkets Dagblad Politken* – then linked to the Swedish Communist Party led by Zeth Högland and Ture Nerman. The first game, taking place on 2 August and against a mix of Stockholm players, ended in a 5–5 draw. Soon after, the Soviets won 4–3 against Fässbersgs IF, an amateur Gothenburg team that would win the Swedish championship the following year.

The Soviet press highlighted its players' good performances. Thus, the official newspaper of the Soviet government, *Izvestia*, explained that 'the performance of our sportspeople does not just have a purely sporting significance. Russian football players are well received everywhere, particularly by workers, with enthusiasm that often acquires the character of an ovation in honour of Soviet Russia'. For its part, the Swedish conservative press openly criticised the home teams' line-ups as, the papers argued, these would ease the chances of victory for the Soviet squad. This, they said, would 'feed Soviet propaganda'. In response to these comments, the head of the Soviet delegation, A. Medvedev – then, the president of the Moscow Council of Physical Culture – sent a letter to the Swedish Football Federation (SvFF) which assured that 'they were not scared of anyone' and that the Soviets could take on any Swedish team. This gesture – widely reported in the Nordic press – led to a new match being played at Stock-

---

of the revolutionary triumph, he became head of Moscow Town Hall's Health Department. In July 1918, he was appointed as the RSFSR Commissar of Health and laid the foundations for the Soviet public health system. Contrary to what Hygienists thought, Semashko was a strong supporter of promoting competition in sport, as, he argued, this 'should serve, ultimately, as a means of involving the masses in the building of socialism'. Riordan, *Sport in Soviet Society*, p. 97.

holm's Royal Stadium. Even though the media advertised it as Sweden vs. Russia, the hosts did not play their national squad to avoid being given a more-than-likely penalisation from FIFA. Actually, the Soviets' rival was a team formed of the best players from the Swedish capital. Expectations were at a fever pitch, and nearly 40,000 spectators filled the stands. Despite pressure from the crowd and the high level of their opponents, the visitors managed to beat the Swedes 1–2, thanks to goals by Pyotr Grigoryev and the captain and star of the team Mikhail Butusov. It was a prestigious win for the new Soviet team, which consisted of players from clubs such as *Krasnaya Presnya* – from Moscow – and Kolomyagi, Sport, Merdzur, Unitas, and Putilovsky Kruzhok – all from Petrograd.

These games the Soviet team played in Sweden should be appreciated because, then, the two countries did not share diplomatic relations. Consequently, football was used to break the international blockade suffered by the USSR, and encourage gaining official recognition and creating bilateral relations with other states. In other words, it served as a tool for Soviet diplomacy.

After the mini-tour in Sweden, the USSR team was given a farewell at Stockholm train station to the tune of the International. Its next destination was Norway. In Oslo on 30 August, the RSFSR squad beat a team made up of players from different local clubs. Again, FIFA rules had prevented the USSR and Norway from openly playing each other. The last stop on the squad's voyage was Estonia, where the Soviets also beat their challengers. The same year, the RSFSR team played two more matches: the first in Szczecin (Poland), against a team formed by workers, and the second in Berlin.

In 1924, a mix of Leningrad footballers played three matches against teams of Finnish, Norwegian, and German workers, which it beat 4–0, 5–3, and 7–1, respectively. That year, however, the Soviet authorities decided to drop their opposition to competing against 'bourgeois' teams. Regarding this, Nikolay Semashko, the first chairman of the Supreme Council of Physical Health, said, '[i]f these matches are useful for Soviet Russia, then we must play them'. Yet this change in attitude came up against an important obstacle: the USSR was not a member of FIFA – and would not be one until 1946. This prevented both the *Sbornaya* and Soviet clubs from playing matches against other national teams or city clubs, as the others would run the risk of penalties.

A suitable rival was needed once the historic decision was made to overcome international isolation by playing against teams from the 'Western capitalist world' that might include professional footballers. A national team that would run the risk of being excluded by FIFA, which was from a kindred state, and, if this were possible, also weak at football to avoid a bitter Soviet debut. In the end, the most convenient solution for Soviet interests was to play against the Republic of Turkey. It was a new state presided over by Mustafa Kemal Atatürk that had emerged from the Turkish War of Independence (1919–1923) and the signing of the Treaty of Lausanne (1923), which had certified the abolition of the Ottoman Empire and the creation of a parliamentary democracy with a Westernising bent. Consequently, the new government used the cult of sport as an educational tool to spread and introduce new modernising values.

It also must be borne in mind that the Bolsheviks also approved of the Atatürk-led revolutionary movement, as they considered it to have similar geopolitical aspirations. It was a perception shared by the Turkish nationalists, who remembered how the Soviets had renounced the historic claims of the Russian Empire over Western Armenia and the Turkish straits. The understanding between both governments was also positively influenced by the Soviet provision of arms and gold to the Turkish revolutionaries at the beginning of the decade, which was a key factor in their success.[6] Finally, we must add that the RSFSR was the second territory to recognise the Kemalist government by means of the Treaty of Moscow, signed on 16 March 1921, according to which both governments committed themselves to developing fraternal relations.

As part of a tour of Europe, the Turkish football team visited Poland, Finland, Estonia, and Latvia. Then, it headed for the URSS but to play in the land of the Soviets, the new Turkish Football Federation (TFF, created in April 1923) needed a special permit from FIFA.

The idea was that the Turks play three matches in the USSR: two against a selection of Moscow players, and a final one against the Soviet national team. In spite of the mutual understanding between the two governments, the Turks' presence in Russia also unleashed angry reactions. Not everyone approved of the USSR playing against representatives of so-called 'bourgeois sport'. In order to counter this strand of thinking, *Pravda* newspaper affirmed that

> our matches against bourgeois sportspeople are necessary and beneficial. They represent an effective means by which to break the blockade imposed by the capitalists. They allow raising the flag of the first workers' and peasants' state in the world, not to hoist them on embassy buildings, but in the hearts and minds of the people. These matches represent the living truth of our country.

---

6   Indeed, one of the leaders of the Young Turks, Enver Pasha, had offered his services to the Bolsheviks when given asylum in Russia.

Lastly, after the Soviet Union participated in the Olympic Games held in Paris in 1924, on 16 November that year, the USSR's national team played its first FIFA-endorsed official match against Turkey. In the earlier matches in Soviet lands, the Turks had won the first against a pick of Moscow players, 1–3, and lost the second 2–1.[7]

In that first official match against a foreign team, the Soviet players wore a red shirt and white pants, a national kit that would last until the collapse of the USSR in 1991. The match, which produced much expectation, was played before 15,000 spectators. Its venue was Moscow's Vorovsky Stadium – ZKS' old ground. This was dedicated to the diplomat and literary critic Vatslav Vorovsky, who had been assassinated a few months before, while representing the Soviet government at the Lausanne Conference (which would end with the signing of the peace Treaty, named after the conference location, that established modern Turkey's borders).

The match – refereed by the Turkish official Hamdi Emin – proved the superiority of the home team. They won 3–0, thanks to their superior individual technique, with Butusov scoring two[8] and Shpakovsky a final goal in the second half.

---

7   In the 1924–1931 period, no other country in the world received as many Soviet sporting delegations as Turkey. In those years, the two countries' football teams played each other as many as ten times. The humiliating pounding suffered by the Finns was not repeated, but the matches against the Turks did not end with easy local victories because the Soviet authorities had told their players to avoid score-lines that would have been offensive to the Turks.

8   A talented footballer with a powerful shot, Mikhail Butusov played for Dinamo Leningrad until 1936, when he hung up his boots at the age of 31. With this team, he won five local championships (1928, 1929, 1931, 1933, and 1935). On several occasions, he captained the Russian team, in whose colours he scored 88 goals. Later, until 1953, he managed the clubs *Dinamo Leningrad*, *Dinamo Tbilisi*, *Dinamo Kiev* – twice – and Zenit Leningrad. He combined playing both football and *bandy* (Russian hockey).

The Soviet eleven, managed by Mikhail Kozlov, was on that day made up of five footballers from Moscow (Sokolov, Ruschinsky, Selin, Isakov, and Shaposhnikov), four from Leningrad (Filippov, Grigoryev, Ezhov, and Butusov), and two from Kharkiv (Shpakovsky and Privalov).

On 15 May 1925, seven months before the USSR and Turkey signed a nonaggression pact, the Soviet team returned Turkey's visit to the Union. Its delegation was received with full honours in Turkey. Nobody could ignore the political backdrop to the *Sbornaya* being there. The Istanbul press reported that 'the match provided a clear example of the strengthening of relations between our two peoples'. Meanwhile, in Western Europe some of the conservative media expressed their disapproval of the Turkish behaviour and castigated FIFA for allowing one of its members to act to spread 'Bolshevik propaganda' and doing so 'scot free'.

To top it all, on match day, the box at Ankara's Shtiklyal Stadium was filled with the country's senior representatives. Attending – as well as 5000 spectators squeezed together in the ground's only stand – was the chair of the Turkish parliament, several ministers, and the Soviet ambassador to the country. They all saw first-hand how the away team came back in the final minutes of the game. A hard-won 1–2 victory, which was much celebrated by the Soviet fans, who received their footballers as 'national heroes'. Even the press joined in the praise, as shown by a *Krasny Sport* (Red Sport) report:

> Definitively the era has passed in which, thanks to a good memory of Tsarism – the tomb of all cultural manifestations – the Soviet country was thought to be a nobody in the sporting field … The match against the Turkish national team in Moscow last year and the one this spring have only confirmed our physical culture's high technical level.

In spite of the step forward made by these contests with Turkey, the fact that the Soviet authorities rejected abandoning the Red Sport International (RSI), as FIFA had called for, meant the prolongation of Soviet football's isolation. In fact, after the mentioned two matches, FIFA threatened the Turkish Federation with severe penalties and, even, expulsion from the international body if Turkey continued to play against the USSR. That explains why these two matches against the 'friendly power' were the *Sbornaya's* only officially recognised ones until the USSR participated in the Helsinki Olympic Games in 1952.

Despite the warnings, both national squads played each other again in 1931. This time, it was presented as a match between two university teams to avoid FIFA reprisals. Indeed, until 1935, the Soviets and the Turks played yearly matches, always using trickery, such as playing under the name 'House of the Turkish People', to avoid violating regulations. They are matches that the Turkish national squad's historical-statistics registry deems to have been played by its 'B team'.

Thanks to the above-mentioned matches, the Soviets were able to discover the tactical evolution undertaken by European football. During the Turks' tour of the USSR in 1933, the visitors put into practice an innovative playing system for the time: known as the 'W', and which prioritised defending by having three players play at the back. For those years, this was a real tactical revolution. The Soviet authorities, however, ignored the changes, adducing that they corresponded to bourgeois football. First and foremost, it was necessary to demonstrate the validity and superiority of the Soviet ways.[9]

---

9   It would take until 1937 and the arrival on the Muscovite *Spartak* bench of Konstantin Pavlovich Kvashin before the 'W' system was put into practice for the first time in Soviet football. Its introduction enabled *Spartak* to be the only team that defeated a specially chosen mix of

During that year and the next, the Soviet national and club teams continued to go on 'missions' abroad. Footballing diplomacy was used to establish paths of understanding with other countries and allow the Soviet Union to break out of its quarantine. In 1926, for instance, the Persian national squad played four matches in Baku (resulting in three home wins and a draw). Relations with the USSR had become normalised after a coup, in 1921, brought to power Reza Pahlavi (who, four years later, anointed himself as Shah of Iran). Football fixtures in which Soviet clubs took on Persian ones were held over three years (1927–1929). Examples include Ashgabat (the club at the capital of the Soviet Socialist Republic of Turkmenistan), which played in the Iranian city of Mashhad, or Baku, which played in Tehran.

In other cases, however, even sport did not manage to help overcome countries' reluctance to engage with Russia. This was so with Czechoslovakia, Poland, and Romania, which avoided establishing relations with the USSR in the cultural and sporting fields. This was despite all of these ratifying (in 1929) what became known as the Litvinov Protocol, to guarantee peace between signatory states.[10]

Two years before, in 1927, a Soviet delegation had travelled to Leipzig (Germany) to compete against a 'German workers' team'. The Soviets beat the home team 8–2 – a score-line that altered the comradely atmosphere prior to the game. Tensions grew and in succeeding matches there were even clashes on

Basque footballers that was doing a tour of the Soviet Union that summer. The prize it was given for this victory was being able to play two international workers' tournaments in Europe and it also had the effect of strengthening the club's popularity.

10   Paradoxically, a decade later, the signing of the German–Soviet Nonaggression Pact – also known as the Molotov–Ribbentrop Pact – did not prevent the German and Soviet football teams from playing each other, as happened both in Germany and the USSR.

the playing field that led to a Soviet player having to leave the pitch with a gash on his head. Instead of repeating the positive scenes from the trip to Sweden, this time the foreign victories were met with a significant silence.

When the tour ended, the German Communists sent a letter to the Central Committee of the Red Sport International to show its displeasure over their rivals' conduct. According to the Germans, the Soviets' rough and aggressive game was more befitting of a bourgeois club than a Communist one. It was underlined that 'they are not doing a good service to the internationalist cause'. Adding to the problem was the turmoil caused by the Soviet players at the hostel they stayed in. Many got drunk and they even punched their own delegation head, who had been accompanying them since they arrived in Germany. Having witnessed the scene, the hosts recommended to the Soviet sporting authorities that '[f]or future trips abroad by Russian sportspeople, please pick as delegation leader a comrade who is firstly a communist and secondly a player'.

The accusations did not stop there because the Germans labelled their Russian 'brothers' as disloyal for having sent a team of professional footballers instead of a workers' team. For their part, the Soviet authorities only acknowledged that it was true that few of its players worked in factories.

Despite the Soviets showing their technical superiority, they suffered a first defeat at the hands of a team of Viennese workers. The Austrians won 3–0 but ironically they were not able to celebrate the victory with their fellow countrypeople because the Austrian government had prohibited the USSR squad from entering its country (in order to avoid infiltration by Communist agents). For that reason, the match ended up being played in the German city of Dresden.

Two days later, a second match was played, which ended in a resounding 1–6 win by the Soviets. Despite scoring so many, when the Russian delegation returned to the USSR, the Supreme Council of Physical Culture ordered its head – Sardakov – to appear before it to explain the Dresden setback. He put this down to his players' tiredness after having played several matches and had an exhausting car ride from Leipzig to the city.

The final sporting balance of that first international experience by the Soviet team in 1927 was nine wins, one draw and a single defeat, with 61 goals for and only 14 against.

16

A Mass Sport in the USSR

Sport – particularly football, and ice hockey during the winter – flourished greatly among the working class in the country's big cities in the first half of the 1920s. In that period, players such as Mikhail Butusov and Fyodor Selin became real household names.

The taking of power by the Bolsheviks shook the world of sport. An example is boxing, which was declared illegal in Leningrad, as it was cited as a health hazard ('as a harmful activity able to incite insane instincts').

Football also remained under suspicion and was subject to big criticisms. These came particularly from members of the above-mentioned *Proletkult*: The Bogdanov-led movement of different cultural associations and avant-garde artists, which aimed to provide a new revolutionary aesthetic.[1] The movement advocated extending practising gymnastics by incorporating it into the working day. On the other hand, it rejected sports such as tennis and football because it saw them as irrelevant or even counter-productive – given the associated

---

1   This was created in July 1917 at the Executive Committee of the Petrograd Soviet's Agitation School and disbanded in 1932. It was linked to the USSR's People's Commissariat for Education even though it always evaded being controlled by the state apparatus. In 1920, it had 84,000 members spread across approximately 300 clubs. Its origins date back to the 1905 revolutionary attempt, the failure of which led some members of the Bolshevik wing of the Russian Social-Democratic Workers' Party (POSDR), such as Anatoly Lunacharsky, to focus on art as a way to inspire revolutionary political action.

risk of injury they had – which could hamper productivity. *Proletkult* was very influential after the October Revolution, and kept its independence in relation to the Party until 1919. It was that year that the movement became tied to the Education Commission, until, in 1925, it was put under the control of the trade unions. Eventually, in 1932, it was disbanded by an official decree.

For the *Proletkultists*, football was 'a game invented by the English bourgeoisie that was intrinsically and morally detrimental: dribbling and dummies, for example, are no more than trickery'. Sport, therefore, was ideologically incompatible with socialist society due to its competitive nature, which reflected the essence of capitalism.

Other criticisms revolved around the financial rewards given to players, which, according to critics, demonstrated football's capitalist sediment.[2] It was also contended that sport was detrimental to young people's health because of the fights that often occurred on pitches and the terraces. Football was even identified with the 'root of evil caused by hankering for victory at any price, something which lowers a sport to being a bloody spectacle'. To avoid this 'violent degeneration', *Proletkult* proposed dividing the pitch into boxes, each of which would be occupied by a player that could not leave this space and would have to pass the ball to a teammate in less than five seconds. That way, physical contact between players would be avoided and, thus, any violent clashes.

To the critics' dismay, the Soviet people wanted to keep football as it had been until then. In spite of the attempts to transform it or even eradicate it, it remained the most popular summer sport – as demonstrated by the previously cited match

2   Precisely for this reason, in 1925, a Disqualification Commission was set up, aiming to 'prevent foul play', at the same time as explicitly prohibiting player transfers.

against Turkey in Moscow. Growing attendance at matches led the authorities to envisage the project for a big stadium to be constructed that might satisfy 'people's extraordinary craving for football'. It also attracted a section of what was called the 'creative intelligentsia'. Russian literature, which historically had been uninterested in football, discovered the sport in that era. This was thanks to authors like Yury Olesha, a Ukrainian writer of Polish origin, who had played as midfielder for Odessa during his college years.[3] In 1926, a poll was even promoted among people to know who was the country's most popular footballer. The winner was the Leningrad goalkeeper Nicolai Sokolov.

Two years later, the Dynamo Stadium was officially opened in Moscow. It was an enormous venue, of modern design – due to its horseshoe shape (open to Petrovsky Park and close to Leningradsky Avenue). It was the work of the architects Arkady Langman and Lazar Tcherykover, and it was built to host the *Spartakiad* events to be held in August that year.

On top of building the appropriate infrastructure, the new authorities engaged in a deep reform of the country's sporting structures. In 1922, many of the earlier clubs, such as Zamoskvoretsky Sports Club (ZKS) and Sokolnichesky Sports Club (SKS), were closed down. In Moscow, control over sport was passed on to the Provincial Council of Physical Culture, a body created by the Provincial Council of Workers, Peasants

---

3   In 1922, after publishing his first work, *Angeli*, Olesha moved to Moscow to work in the newsroom of a popular newspaper, where he wrote satirical poems under the pseudonym Зубило (Zubilo; the Chisel). In the 1930s, the Starostin brothers included him in the advisory board for the Spartak Moscow coaches, alongside the actor Mikhail Yanshin and the sports journalist Lev Kassil. Andrey Starostin, a personal friend of Olesha, recalled that the writer would boast of having been the first to bestow football with 'literary dignity' in the Soviet Union.

and Deputies. The same also happened in Petrograd and the major Ukrainian cities and towns.

This whole series of reforms took place during the shift from what was called 'bourgeois football' to 'proletarian football'. In this process – set in motion in the 1920s and coinciding with football's popularisation in the country – the pre-revolutionary clubs were compulsorily linked to the authorities, state firms, the security forces or the army. This was the case with CDKA (the Central House of the Red Army), formed in 1928 and which in 1960 would be renamed CSKA (the Central Sports Club of the Army). The military team benefited from the 'nationalisation' – in April 1923 – of the facilities of the Amateur Society of Skiing Sports (OLLS), which had won the Muscovite football championship the year before. From that time, football was officially adopted by the army as a 'compulsory training activity'.

In that period, membership of any sports society was based on the profession of the associate or player. Therefore, while soldiers played in the Red Army teams, Interior Ministry employees played for Dynamo, transport union members for *Lokomotiv*, car-manufacturing workers for *Torpedo*, and aeronautical-industry workers for *Krylya Sovetov* (Soviet Wings).

On 24 June 1923, the Dynamo Proletarian Sports Society was founded. It was an initiative of Felix Dzerzhinsky, People's Commissar for Domestic Affairs and director of the State Political Directorate (GPU) – the secret police operating in the country from 1922 to 1924 and created out of the Cheka;[4] and the only club that escaped the control of the Supreme Council of Physical Culture. For Dzerzhinsky, it was vital that his men did sport, as it would enable them to develop

4   For that reason, Dzerzhinsky was made the club's honorary president.

'strength, dexterity, courage and endurance'.[5] Little by little, the club would normalise its situation until it became a sports club like the others, progressively opening it up to other security-agency staff, border guards, and their relatives. In no time, different sections of the club were created across the country. By October 1923, it had 36 branches and new sporting activities were added to the existing ones – to eventually include football, basketball, wrestling, jiu-jitsu, gymnastics, shooting, fencing, and boxing. This meant that Dynamo became the first big multi-sports club in the Soviet Union.

The backbone of the Dynamo structure was the Sokolniki Football Players' Circle (KFS). The state-security-linked team played its first official match – a Moscow League game – on 17 June 1923. Its opponent was *Krasnaya Presnya*[6] – the Starostin

---

5 Riordan, *Sport in Soviet Society*, p. 94.
6 The team took the name of the neighbourhood in which it was created, Presnya – itself named after the Moskva River tributary. It stood out for being one of the Moscow districts with the most active revolutionary membership. In the late eighteenth century, the area became one of Moscow's industrial epicentres. In 1799, the first Russian textile factory, Trekhgornaya Manufaktura, was introduced there. This encouraged the local creation of left political organisations: social-democratic ones from September 1894 to 1895; the Socialist Revolutionaries (SRs) years later; and the Bolsheviks from September 1917. In 1900, the neighbourhood had 135,000 residents – of which 70 per cent were of peasant origin – and around seventy factories, such as the Danilovsky sugar refinery, Dukat Tobacco, the Shmidt furniture maker, and the Prokhorov plant. Presnya emerged as one of the main centres of the armed uprising in December 1905, for which it was shelled by state artillery. Nearly a thousand civilians were killed. After the triumph of the October Revolution, the district was renamed Krasnaya Presnya to honour the workers that led the 1905 insurrectionary attempt. Later, Presnya workers played an active role in the forming of a Soviet government in Moscow. In fact, Lenin was the deputy representing Presnya's workers in the city's Soviet. As well as its rebellious disposition, the area was also characterised by acts of hooliganism, petty theft, and cheap prostitution. In such a context, football – together with reading detective novels – offered local young

brothers' team[7] – that in 1935 took on its final name of Spartak Moscow.

Another club that felt the effects of the Revolution was *Kazanka*. This was founded in 1910 by workers from the locomotive depot at Kazansky railway station. In 1922, it registered for the Muscovite league and, in December 1935, the People's Commissar for Transport, Lazar Kaganovich, approved its new name: *Lokomotiv*. The Moscow railway workers' team would play its official debut on 6 May 1936.

Finally, in September 1923, the first Soviet football championship started. The body responsible for organising it was the *Vsesojuznaja Sekcija Futbola* (Pan-Soviet Football Section). In the league, there were representatives from different towns and cities in the USSR's federated republics. The tournament did not enjoy regularity, as shown by the fact that the second edition was not played until 1928. This was within the first *Spartakiad*, held in Moscow, and in which 17 countries par-

people an alternative to drinking and taking drugs, gambling, trips to brothels, mass fights on the banks of the Moskva River, or criminal activity. Indeed, the area was 'so dangerous even to its lower-class inhabitants that police permitted workers at the Mamontov varnish factory near the Presnya [sic] Gates, to carry guns for self-protection' – remembered in Edelman, *Spartak Moscow*, p. 29.

7 The other great footballing dynasty from the Presnya neighbourhood was that of the Artemyev brothers: Ivan, Sergei, and Pyotr. Ivan, the oldest of them, was one of the organisers of the first matches to be played in the district. Concretely, he was invited to play with the Presnya Society of Physical Education (OFV). This was under the orders of coach Boris Efimovich Evdokimov, who combined managing the team with underground Bolshevik activism. In 1914, Ivan Artemyev was called up to fight for the Imperial Army, in which he served for two years. In February 1917, he returned to Presnya and committed himself to the Bolshevik cause, for which he was imprisoned by the Provisional Government, but freed during the October Revolution. Later, Artemyev remained linked to football, being one of the promoters of Krasnaya Presnya and involved in the construction of its first stadium.

ticipated. That very year had seen the official opening of the Dynamo Stadium, which would end up having a capacity of 50,000 spectators. That confirmed the strong following for Soviet football in the late 1920s, which by the early years of the next decade would become a genuine mass phenomenon. This growth also was possible thanks to a series of tours that the country's main teams carried out in the second half of the twenties. This was how football spread to Central Asia and the Caucus, for example.[8]

In those years, football aroused passions in the Soviet Union, but it still was a restricted sport, as going to a match was a real treat and not due to its cost, which was still relatively cheap.[9] Rather, getting tickets was reserved for those that supposedly had earned a treat at their particular factory. The factory committees were those responsible for allotting tickets among employees. Soviet elite football began to create its own stars – idols that produced admiration among the youngest and attracted huge crowds to the stadiums.

All these factors explain football's expansion across the country. The years in which access to playing it was limited were a distant memory. With the triumph of the Revolution,

8   Those tours, however, meant that the players would leave their workplaces for months and lose their corresponding wages, meaning they would need to be financially compensated. This happened at a time in which the professional game – identified with bourgeois capitalism – was held up as the antithesis of the society being promoted in the Soviet Union. The USSR's first professional league was not played until 1936. We have an example in the Spartak Moscow players: the Starostin brothers Andrey and Nikolay, who worked repairing tractors; another brother, Aleksandr, who was an employee at the Tomsky Stadium; Pyotr Isakov, who was a wage earner at the Dukat tobacco factory; and Pavel Kanunnikov, who was a sales assistant at a sportswear shop.

9   The price of a covered standing ticket would be 45 kopeks: a manageable amount in the later 1920s and cheaper than a theatre or picture-house ticket.

football became democratised until it became a true mass sport of the young Soviet Union. Its size, however, also led to business arising in relation to it. Although professionalism was prohibited, a kind of 'football black market' emerged in the twenties. Club heads took advantage of lax regulations to try to sign the best talent from other teams.

The country's new authorities understood football's potential. All the same, the sport's growth, as well as the privileges and money surrounding it, aroused some consternation among members of the government – in particular, Ministers of Education, Health, Defence, and Interior.[10] Many of the Leninist intellectuals were also wary of the spontaneity of 'the uneducated fan masses'. For such thinkers, when football was watched from the stands rather than played, it was something dangerous: 'an irrational and uncontrollable spectacle that aroused emotions and often ended in violence'.[11] Footballers did not escape criticism, as they were seen to be enjoying too many privileges and financial rewards. Despite repeated attempts to avoid professionalism, football became consolidated as a business from 1928 onwards.

Beyond its educational benefits, football acted as a social glue for the USSR's heterogeneous ethnic and cultural mosaic. This was possible because it had a great advantage over literature, theatre and other cultural expressions: it was

---

10   To nip any signs of professionalism in the bud, the Muscovite authorities decided to reorganise local football in 1926. Around the country, the old sporting structures were replaced and, from then, clubs had to be linked to a union or factory. Only the police and army teams were exempt from complying with these new rules. From 1930 onwards, control of sporting activity rested with the All-Union Council of Physical Culture (VSFK) – a body run by sportspersons committed to Bolshevism. These included Lev Kamenev and Genrikh Yagoda, as well as the general secretary of the Central Committee of the Komsomol, Aleksandr Kosarev.

11   Edelman, *Spartak Moscow*, p. 57.

easier for the masses to understand it. Hence, its enormous popularity among the Soviet urban proletariat in the period.

Being left behind, then, were the 'bearded faces and nickel-plated glasses of the revolutionary period'.[12] The Revolution's triumph meant the rise of the citizen and the spread of the 'new Soviet man' ideal[13] in order to overcome the idle *homo sapiens* – to use Trotsky's words. The new citizen was characterised by his or her altruistic collectivism: quite different from the individualistic selfishness of bourgeois capitalist societies and a prototype that held up athletic youth as a benchmark. In the case of football, those directing it promoted – from the 1920s onwards – the figure of the goalkeeper (*vratar*), who gradually emerged as the 'prime symbolic defender' of the Soviet state. Seen as the first line of defence, the goalkeeper was exalted as a national hero who symbolised protecting the country from attack by the opposing team – a real and understandable metaphor for the country's military defence.[14] This, thus,

12 F. Veiga, P. Martín, and J. Sánchez Monroe, *Entre dos octubres. Revoluciones y contrarrevoluciones en Rusia (1905–1917) y guerra civil en Eurasia* (Madrid: Alianza Editorial, 2017), p. 592.

13 The new Soviet man of the thirties aimed to be a more developed version than its predecessor, embodying the ideal set of qualities at that time: clean, healthy and politically intelligent. His new characteristics were resistance, perseverance, and the ability to control one's own and other people's emotions.

14 The figure of the goalkeeper became a Socialist symbol, which explains why it features in a multitude of creative works – from books to paintings. In the novel *Envy* by journalist Yury Olesha, the values of the new Soviet man – shown through the young goalkeeper Volodya Makarov – are contrasted with those of Western citizens. Other works include *Vratar* by painter and poster-illustrator Aleksandr Deyneka, one of the most significant artists in the field of socialist realism; or the film of the same name by director Semen Timoshenko, which premiered in 1939. Its screenplay was written by Lev Kassil, who also worked as journalist for *Izvestia*, and was based on Kassil's book *The Goalkeeper of the Republic* – published a year before.

allows us to comprehend even more the renown enjoyed at the time by Lev Yashin: the world's only goalkeeper to have been given the *Ballon d'Or* (for best European player) – awarded by *France Football* magazine in 1963.

Epilogue

Soccer's arrival in Russia coincided with the final period of Tsarist rule. The sport was associated with the foreign-settler community and locals' access to clubs remained restricted – a situation criticised by the well-to-do Russians who were passionate about a sport they saw as synonymous with modernity. In contrast, some of the elites rejected football precisely because of its alien origin. Consequently, the Russian ruling class vacillated in its attitude to football, swaying between enthusiasm and incendiary disrespect.

Furthermore, the existing clubs were part of the lifestyles associated with the bourgeoisie and aristocracy. And, evidently, the working class was initially excluded from the sport. This was not just because workers could not afford to pay prohibitive membership fees or competition fees. They also were refused membership due to their social origins. Such extremes explain why all over Europe social-democratic parties, such as the German SDP, tried to provide the chances for physical recreation that capitalism was failing to give workers and peasants. These obstacles to engaging in sport partly explain the hostility the socialist rank-and-file had towards mass sport. Indeed, socialists saw sport as one of the main expressions of modern nationalism, whose aim merely was to produce – in the writer Maxim Gorky's words– cannon fodder for imperialist wars. As we have noted, sport's harshest critics added that practising sport diverted workers away from political engagement. Yet despite their initial distance, revolutionaries would end up promoting sport – driven to do so by the demands of war.

The fact is that football spread among the Russian labour movement in an unusual way, with the aim of ending one of the country's still-endemic problems: alcoholism. Work absenteeism caused by excessive drinking encouraged factory owners to consent to football being introduced in the workplace. The sport would keep employees entertained and away from the vodka. The Charnock brothers set the example and other factory managers and owners soon followed suit. This was how football became popularised and years later became a mass sport.

After its introduction and the broadening of its class base, football was shaken up once again by the triumph of the October Revolution. The creation of new authorities led to the replacement of Russian football's power structures – until then in non-Russian hands. Flight by foreign residents – fearful of the effects of the uprising – led Russians to take charge of the institutions that oversaw the national game. Thus, a reverberation of the Bolsheviks' rise to power was the 'nationalisation' of Russian football – until then in British and German hands.

Russia's revolutionary leaders had been reticent towards the Western sporting model, which they labelled as capitalist. Now they were impelled to impose compulsory physical education for young people – including in schools. The reason for this was the Russian Civil War, which threatened to liquidate the fledgling socialist state. Paradoxically the Bolshevik leaders – in some cases reluctantly – had to follow the old regime's steps and promote military-orientated physical training among the population. Consequently the war brought about the spread of sport across the whole country.

Meanwhile, the new leaders began to take advantage of sport – through mass parades such as those held in Moscow's Red Square – as a way to promote and legitimise the new socialist state. They went from holding an unorganised May Day celebration in Moscow in 1918 to the staging – two years later – of the storming of the Winter Palace to celebrate its third anniversary. The latter event involved 10,000 disciplined participants. The first uniquely sporting exhibition had been held the previous year to celebrate the first birthday of Vsevobuch, the Central Board for Universal Military Training. On 25 May 1919, in the middle of the Civil War, a large contingent of athletes paraded in Red Square in the presence of Lenin and Trotsky – attending as head of the Red Army. Clearly the backdrop to the event was none other than promoting militarised sporting practise among Soviet youth, and thereby increasing their physical training for the war.

As mentioned, the war (and the emergencies it created) paradoxically spurred the revolutionary authorities to promote sport. Those leaders that hitherto were reticent about the spread of what they deemed to be a pastime of industrial capitalism, now changed their mind and advocated extending physical education to the whole country.

The Soviet leaders used sport and particularly football to pursue two goals: first, to show the world the USSR's strength; and, second, to help the country overcome its international isolation. Between 1926 and 1937, as well as its yearly matches against Turkey, the Soviet team and different city sides played against workers' teams from Austria, England, Germany, Norway, Czechoslovakia, and Sweden. Football both acted as a vanguard for Soviet diplomacy and a transmission belt for internationalism. *Sbornaya* and club matches were used to normalise relations with states bordering the USSR. As well as establishing neighbourly relations, the aim was to demonstrate the virtues and strength of the socialist state through a powerful exhibition of football. This would prove the superiority of the socialist model in relation to bourgeois sport. Accordingly, victories would be analysed in political terms and exploited using propaganda demonstrating the supremacy of the Soviet system.

Others also instrumentalised football and for different purposes. Its expansion to almost all of the Soviet Republics was meant to unite the heterogeneous mosaic of ethnicities and cultures that made up the USSR. But in some territories the game became a focus for anti-Russian animosity. In certain Central Asian Republics, some Muslim councils used soccer to disseminate their proclamations among local people: 'Look, the Russians have brought the devil's head [referring to the ball]. See how it brings misfortune.'[1] Even so, in Moscow, sport and particularly football was perceived to be 'the only chance of unifying flags, ideologies and sentiment'.[2]

In the early 1930s and accompanying the First Five-Year Plan (1928–1932), the authorities began promoting physical education again. On 11 March 1931, the Supreme Council of Physical Culture – on the Komsomol's initiative – launched a new era of *fizkultura*. This included the programme Ready for Labour and the Defence of the USSR – popularly known by its Russian acronym GTO. This extended training, addressed to all citizens (divided into three age groups) but focused on giving patriotic education through sport to Soviet youth.[3]

---

1   Riordan, *Sport in Soviet Society*, p. 114.

2   J. C. Fernández Truán, 'El movimiento gimnástico del Este (2.ª parte)', p. 18.

3   In 1939, in the build-up to war, new physical tests were introduced to prepare young people to serve in the Red Army. These included quick-step marching, swimming, rifle shooting, and hand-grenade throwing, and even practising martial arts and learning first aid. Most of the tests, apart from that of grenade throwing and rifle shooting – both restricted to males – were scrapped after the Second World War. In 2013, Russian President Vladimir Putin publicly stated that reintroducing the GTO

The GTO was designed to take account of 'the dual demands of developing industrial productivity and military might'.[4] Through generalising sport, the aim was to train future workers and soldiers and improve their relative physical abilities. A clear illustration of militarism's ascendancy at the time was that the first recipients of training were officers from Moscow's prestigious Frunze Military Academy. (The school was named so in homage to Mikhail Vasilyevich Frunze, the Bolshevik leader during the October Revolution who died in mysterious circumstances in 1925 – the year he was made Chair of the Revolutionary Military Council.)

Under the guidance of the VSFK (Supreme Council of Physical Culture), football was restructured at the beginning of the 1930s. One of the measures implemented was to make it obligatory for footballers to be workers in the factories or members of the unions, which gave the respective teams their name. This decision led to the disintegration of the smaller clubs, who could not keep their players. This was to the advantage of teams such as Dynamo or TsDKA (CSKA), the army team, which had the ideal structure to incorporate the best players at the time.

The first professional league competition was held on 22 May 1936 – the year the USSR's Constitution was passed at the Eighth Special Congress of the Soviets. The league included 28 teams, seven of which would play in the highest tier ('Group A'). Soon after, Stalin began the Great Purge: his strategy to repress the so-called 'counter-revolutionary elements and enemies of the people'.

programme would help children 'defend themselves, their family, and ultimately their motherland' ('Vladimir Putin Calls for Revival of Soviet-Era Physical Fitness Tests', *The Telegraph*, 13 March 2013).

4   O'Mahony, *Sport in the USSR*, p. 126.

Holding the first League Championship increased football's popularity in the USSR. Match attendance grew notably, confirming that football had become a truly mass phenomenon, with the two great Muscovite teams – Dynamo and Spartak – striving for hegemony.[5] Rivalry between them would intensify in the thirties when football became a lucrative business with full-time managers, big revenues from ticket sales, and financial rewards for footballers (such as earning bonuses if they won titles). This context assisted the emergence of star players like the Starostin brothers, who were idolised by thousands of supporters. It was in those years that the antagonism between Dynamo and *Spartak* spilt beyond the sporting arena. The authorities preferred citizens to support Dynamo: 'the guardians of order and examples of official values'.[6] Yet Spartak had the biggest following, which contributed to the myth of it being 'the people's team' (despite its clear links with part of the *nomenklatura*). Many of its supporters referred to Dynamo as the club that 'represented the authority – the police, and the organs of state security. The hated privileged elites';[7] an enmity that was also extended to the army's TsDKA. From then, the rivalry turned into hostility. Spats and fights, both on the pitch and off, would replace the previous brotherhood.

In short, football became a notable transformative element in a turbulent socio-political context. During Tsarism it was founded as a modernising driver of society, aided by the industrialisation process. Both the 1905 Revolution, coinciding with the progressive spread of the sport among the popular classes and particularly the 1917 victory helped football Russify. In

5 For their merits, both clubs were awarded the Lenin Order, which was given to them on 22 July 1937.

6 In Edelman, *Spartak Moscow*, p. 93.

7 Ibid., p. 94.

turn this helped the national unification of the mosaic of ethnicities and cultures that made up the emerging Soviet Union. The world's first socialist state tried to overcome the isolation to which it was subject by the international powers, using football as a spearhead for its diplomacy. At the same time, the game was exploited to convey the inherent ethical, moral, and patriotic values of the 'new Soviet man', which was held up as a model that would demonstrate the supremacy of socialism over capitalism.

Having become a mass phenomenon in the USSR in the twenties, football was used by its Communist leaders to extol socialism's social conquests and successes. For that reason, the authorities side-lined physical-culture programmes, prioritising the link between recreation and public health. The alternative model they promoted was based on covert amateur competitiveness. The best example in the area of football was the aforementioned rivalry between *Spartak* and Dynamo – a real social metaphor for the contrast in the USSR between those that chose to identify with the power structure and those that opted for criticism and dissidence.

Far from being a simple pastime, once associated with the bourgeoisie, football in the Soviet Union became an engine of modernisation, transformation, and cohesion. By surveying the sport's historical evolution, we can reconstruct and understand the dynamics that led to the fall of the biggest empire in the nineteeth century, as well as the advent of the world's first socialist state.

Bibliography

BOOKS

Arnaud, P., and Riordan, J. (1998). *Sport and International Politics. The Impact of Fascism and Communism on Sport* (London: E & F Spon)

Avis, G. (1987). *The Making of the Soviet Citizen: Character Formation and Civic Training in Soviet Education* (London: Croom Helm)

Baker, K. (2015). *Fathers of Football: Great Britons Who Took the Game to the World* (Durrington: Pitch Publishing)

Biggart, J., Gloveli, G., and Yassour, A. (1998) *Bogdanov and his work. A guide to the published and unpublished Works of Alexander A. Bogdanov (Malinovsky) 1873-1928* (London: Routledge)

Bonnell, V. E. (1983) *Roots of Rebellion. Workers' Politics and Organizations in St. Petersburg and Moscow, 1900-1914* (Berkeley: University of California Press)

Clark, K., Dobrenko, E., Artizov, A., and Naumov, O. (2007) *Soviet Culture and Power. A History in Documents, 1917-1953* (New Haven: Yale University Press)

Collins, T. (2013) *Sport in Capitalist Society. A Short History* (Oxford: Routledge)

Curletto, M. A. (2010) *I piedi dei Soviet. Il futból dalla Rivoluzione d'Ottobre alla morte di Stalin* (Genoa: Il Melangolo)

— (2014) *Spartak Mosca. Storie di calcio e potere nell'URSS di Stalin* (Rome: Fila 37)

Curletto, M. A., and Lupi, R. (2014) *Jašin. Vita di un portiere* (Genoa: Il Melangolo)

Downing, D. (1999) *Passovotchka. Moscow Dynamo in Britain, 1945* (London: Bloomsbury Publishing)

Edelman, R. (1993) *Serious Fun: A History of Spectator Sports in the USSR* (Oxford: Oxford University Press)

— (2009) *Spartak Moscow: A History of the People's Team in the Workers' State* (New York: Cornell University Press)

Figes, O. (2010) *La Revolución Rusa (1891–1924). La tragedia de un pueblo* (Barcelona: Edhasa)

— (2012) *Crimea. La primera gran guerra* (Barcelona: Edhasa)

Fontana, J. (2017) *El siglo de la revolución. Una historia del mundo desde 1914* (Barcelona: Crítica)

Gammelsaeter, H., and Senaux, B. (2011) *The Organisation and Governance of Top Football Across Europe: An Institutional Perspective* (New York: Routledge)

Gavrilin, V. (1973) *Sportsmen of the Soviet Army* (Moscow: Novosti Press Agency Publishing House)

Gökay, B. (2006) *Soviet Eastern Policy and Turkey, 1920–1991. Soviet Foreign Policy, Turkey and Communism* (London: Routledge)

Goldblatt, D. (2006) *The Ball is Round. A Global History of Soccer* (London: Viking Penguin)

González Aja, T. (2002) *Sport y autoritarismos. La utilización del deporte por el comunismo y el fascismo* (Madrid: Alianza Editorial)

Grant, S. (2013) *Physical Culture and Sport in Soviet Society. Propaganda, Acculturation and Transformation in the 1920s and 1930s* (New York: Routledge)

Gutmann, A. (2004) *Sports: The First Five Millennia* (Amherst: University of Massachusetts Press)

Hoberman, J. M. (1984) *Sport and Political Ideology* (Austin: University Texas Press)

Katzer, N., Budy, S., Köhring, A., and Zeller, M. (eds., 2010) *Euphoria and Exhaustion. Modern Sport in Soviet Culture and Society* (New York: Campus)

Kruger, A., and Riordan, J. (1996) *The Story of Worker Sport* (Leeds: Human Kinetics)

Lavalette, M. (ed., 2013) *Capitalism and Sport: Politics, Protest, People and Play* (London: Bookmarks Publications)

Leiva Ardana, J. (2012) *Fútbol y Dictaduras. Resistencia vs Propaganda* (Simat de la Valldigna: La Xara Edicions)

Lockhart, B. (1948) *Memorias de un agente británico en Rusia* (Madrid: Ediciones Pegaso)

Louis, V., and Louis, J. (1980) *Sport in the Soviet Union* (Oxford: Pergamon Press)

Mason, T. (1980) *Association Football and English Society, 1863-1915* (Brighton: Harvester Press)

Mawdsley, E. (2017) *Blancos contra rojos. La Guerra Civil rusa* (Madrid: Desperta Ferro Ediciones)

Milosevich, M. (2017) *Breve historia de la Revolución Rusa* (Barcelona: Galaxia Gutenberg)

McReynolds, L. (2002) *Russia at Play: Leisure Activities at the End of the Tsarist Era* (New York: Cornell University Press)

Morgan, K., Cohen, G., and Flinn, A. (eds., 2005) *Agents of Revolution: New Biographical Approaches to the History of International Communism in the Age of Lenin and Stalin* (Bern: Peter Lang Publishing)

Morton, H. W. (1963) *Soviet Sport. Mirror of Soviet Society* (New York: Collier Books)

Murray, B. (1998) *The World's Game: A History of Soccer* (Champaign: University of Illinois Press)

Nauright, J., and Wiggins, D. K. (eds.) (2015) *Sport and Revolutionaries. Reclaiming the Historical Role of Sport in Social and Political Activism* (New York: Routledge)

Nolte, C. E. (2002) *The Sokol in the Czech Lands to 1914: Training for the Nation* (New York: Palgrave Macmillan)

O'Mahony, M. (2006) *Sport in the USSR. Physical Culture – Visual Culture* (London: Reaktion Books)

Peppard, V., and Riordan, J. (1993) *Playing Politics: Soviet Sport Diplomacy to 1992* (Greenwich: JAI Press)

Perel, A. (1958) *Football in the USSR* (Moscow: Foreign Languages Publishing House)

Pipes, R. (2001) *Communism. A History* (New York: Modern Library Chronicles)

Pomyalovsky, N. G. (1973) *Seminary Sketches* (New York: Cornell University Press)

Radzinsky, E. (1993) *El Último Zar* (Barcelona: Plaza & Janés)

Reese, R. R. (2000) *The Soviet Military Experience. A History of the Soviet Army, 1917–1991* (London: Routledge)

Rieber, A. (1982) *Merchants and Entrepreneurs in Imperial Russia* (Chapel Hill: University of North Carolina Press)

Riordan, J. (1977) *Sport in Soviet Society. Development of Sport and Physical Education in Russia and the USSR* (London: Cambridge University Press)

— (1982) *Sport Under Communism: The USSR, Czechoslovakia, the GDR, China, Cuba* (Montreal: McGill – Queen's University Press)

— (1991) *Sport, Politics and Communism* (Manchester: Manchester University Press)

Salvador, J. L. (2004) *El deporte en Occidente. Historia, cultura y política* (Madrid: Cátedra)

Shteĭnbakh, V. (comp., 1987) *Soviet Sport. The Success Story* (Moscow: Raduga Publishers)

Smith, M. (2011) *Six: The Real James Bonds 1909–1939* (London: Biteback Publishing)

Soltis, A. (2000) *Soviet Chess 1917–1991* (Jefferson: McFarland & Company)

Steinberg, D. A. (1979) *Sport Under Red Flags: The Relations Between the Red Sport International and the Socialist Workers' Sport International, 1920-1939*, doctoral thesis (Madison: University of Wisconsin)

Thorpe, A. (2000) *The British Communist Party and Moscow, 1920–43* (Manchester: Manchester University Press)

Veiga, F. (2006) *El turco. Diez siglos a las puertas de Europa* (Barcelona: Debate)

Veiga, F., Martín, P., and Sánchez Monroe, J. (2017) *Entre dos octubres. Revoluciones y contrarrevoluciones en Rusia (1905–1917) y guerra civil en Eurasia* (Madrid: Alianza Editorial)

Vujosevic, T. (2017) *Modernism and the Making of the Soviet New Man* (Manchester: Manchester University Press)

Zelnik, R. E. (1971). *Labor and Society in Tsarist Russia: The Factory Workers of St. Petersburg, 1855-1870* (Palo Alto: Stanford University Press)

ARTICLES

(1982) 'The Finnish Workers' Sports Federation (TUL)', *International Review for the Sociology of Sport*, vol. 17, no. 3 (1 September), pp. 123–125.

Apostolov, A. (2014) 'The Enemy at the Gate: The Soviet Goalkeeper in Cinema, Culture and Policy', *Studies in Russian and Soviet Cinema*, vol. 8, no. 3 (September), pp. 200–217.

Bravo, C. (2017) 'Octubre Rojo en Orekhovo', *Panenka*, no. 68 (November), pp. 82–85.

Elwood, C. (2010) 'The Sporting Life of V. I. Lenin', *Canadian Slavonic Papers / Revue Canadienne des Slavistes*, vol. 52, no. 1–2 (March–June), pp. 79–94.

Fernández Truán, J. C. (2008) 'El movimiento gimnástico del Este (2.ª parte)', *Apunts. Educación Física y Deportes*, no. 93, pp. 12–18.

Frykholm, P. A. (1997). 'Soccer and Social Identity in Pre-Revolutionary Moscow', *Journal of Sport History*, vol. 24, no.2 (Summer), pp. 143–154.

Gounot, A. (1995). 'Els orígens del moviment esportiu comunista a Europa', *Acàcia*, no. 4, pp. 75–99.

— (2000) 'Sport or Political Organization? Structures and Characteristics of the Red Sport International, 1921–1937', *Journal of Sport History*, vol. 28, no. 1, pp. 23–39.

Haynes, J. (2007) 'Film as Political Football: The Goalkeeper', *Studies in Russian and Soviet Cinema*, vol. 1, no. 3, August, pp. 283–297.

Karpov, M. (2017) 'Упражнения с бревном' (Exercises with the Balance Beam), *Lenta.ru*, 15 June.

Keys, B. (2009) 'The Body as a Political Space: Comparing Physical Education under Nazism and Stalinism', *German History*, vol. 25, no. 3, pp. 395–413.

O'Mahony, M. (2016). 'The Art of Goalkeeping: Memorializing Lev Yashin', *Sport in Society*, vol. 20, no. 5–6 (March), pp. 1–19.

Pato, I. (2017) 'Soviets en pantalón corto: de Lenin a la cibernética', *PlayGround*, 12 November.

Riordan, J. (1974) 'Soviet Sport and Soviet Foreign Policy', *Soviet Studies*, vol. 26, no. 3 (July), pp. 322–343.

— (1993) 'Rewriting Soviet Sports History', *Journal of Sports History*, vol. 20, no. 3, Winter.

— (1994) 'The Strange Story of Nikolai Starostin, Football and Lavrentii Beria', *Europe-Asia Studies*, vol. 46, no. 4, pp. 681–690.

— (2007) 'The Impact of Communism on Sport', *Historical Social Research*, no. 32, pp. 110–115.

Rowley, A. (2006) 'Sport in the Service of the State: Images of Physical Culture and Soviet Women, 1917–1941', *The International Journal of the History of Sport*, vol. 23, no. 8, pp. 1314–1340.

Simón, L. (2007) 'Lenin jugava a futbol?', *L'Esportiu*, 15 November, pp. 3–4.

Steinberg, D. A. (1978). 'The Workers' Sport Internationals 1920–28', *Journal of Contemporary History*, vol. 13, no. 2 (April), pp. 233–251.

Usall, R. (2017) 'El club de la revolució', *L'Esportiu*, 18 November.

— (2018) 'Amb molta història', *L'Esportiu*, 26 May.

MEDIA CONSULTED

L'Esportiu
Marca
Panenka
PlayGround

The Guardian
The Telegraph

SPECIALIST JOURNALS

Acàcia
Apunts. Educación Física y Deportes
Canadian Slavonic Papers / Revue Canadienne des Slavistes
Europe-Asia Studies
German History
Historical Social Research
International Review for the Sociology of Sport
Journal of Contemporary History
Journal of Sport History
Soccer & Society
Soviet Studies
Sport History Review
Sport in Society
Studies in Russian and Soviet Cinema
The American Historical Review
The International Journal of the History of Sport

Index

Thanks to our Patreon subscribers:

Andrew Perry
Ciaran Kane

Who have shown generosity and
comradeship in support of our publishing.

Check out the other perks you get by subscribing
to our Patreon – visit patreon.com/plutopress.

Subscriptions start from £3 a month.

The Pluto Press Newsletter

Hello friend of Pluto!

Want to stay on top of the best radical books we publish?

Then sign up to be the first to hear about our new books, as well as special events, podcasts and videos.

You'll also get 50% off your first order with us when you sign up.

Come and join us!

Go to bit.ly/PlutoNewsletter